Praise for
The Mystical Symphony

"In *The Mystical Symphony: A Memoir of Healing, Vision, and Wonder*, Judith E. Bowen tells the story of her life with a profound sense of wonder and gratitude, yet she unflinchingly describes her experiences of pain, and sadness as well. She remembers an early experience of sitting in a church by herself and becoming aware of what she calls a "Presence." That mystical experience led her, spiritually speaking, far from her German Lutheran roots to the work of the twelfth century mystic, Hildegard von Bingen, and many others. Professionally and personally, Judy engages deeply with everyone she meets, learning and growing. To read this book is to be invited into a world of searching and discovery, always with a new horizon just ahead."

DOUGLAS J. BROUWER
Presbyterian pastor and the author of several books, most recently his memoir, *Chasing After Wind: A Pastor's Life* (Eerdmans)

"This heartfelt story, covering eight decades, allows us to follow the path of a wise healer who, despite facing many challenges in life, including loss and disappointment, never lost her faith in the mystical. The book speaks of the solace and healing she's brought to many, touching our hearts with her humility."

CHRISTINE PAGE, MD
Author of *Frontiers of Health*

"*The Mystical Symphony* by Judith Bowen is a profound journey of self-discovery, beautifully weaving a connection to the mystic and healer with a deep reverence for the natural world. It resonates with the universal longing for belonging, the solace of stillness, and the transformative magic of music. Enfolded in luminous, transcendent energy, this book captures the divine moments that shape and uplift our lives."

REBECCA BEARDSALL
Author of *The Unfurling Frond*

the MYSTICAL *symphony*

A MEMOIR OF HEALING, VISION, AND WONDER.

JUDITH E. BOWEN

atmosphere press

For Mary and Katharine
Source of all joy through their gifts of
wisdom, creativity, and wonder

"Stories move in circles,
They don't go in straight lines. So, it helps if you listen in circles.
There are stories inside stories and stories between stories
And finding your way through them is as easy and as hard as
Finding your way home.
And part of the finding is the getting lost.
And when you're lost, you start to look around
And to listen."

Lay Chaplain's Notebook - Module Three: Pastoral Identity

IN THE BEGINNING

At least it's not raining, I think as we leave for the church, the last of March going out pretty much like a lamb. Daddy is happy to take me this late. It gives him a reason to drive our almost-new car, our first car ever. We don't talk much, but that's usual, and it gives me time to think about this night. I knew I wanted to do this as soon as the minister asked for volunteers who would agree to spend an hour sitting in the church on Maundy Thursday to be with Christ. He said people needed to be there all through the night. The earliest spot open when I went to sign up was from eleven to twelve o'clock at night. I was grateful that Daddy was eager to drive.

I'm not sure when the pull to be part of this night started. Was it hearing the church readings leading up to Easter, although I had heard them all for years? Now, a few months into my fifteenth year, I knew them well. Was it when I found myself sketching Christ on the cross soon after I started an art class at the Baum Art School? I felt somehow connected to that man I was sketching. The image emerged from my own imagination. I felt his pain. It was an intensely personal feeling. I really don't know. I just needed to be there with Him.

Daddy pulls up to the church to let me out at the door. "I'll be back at 12:00," he says and drives off.

I walk through the familiar red doors and into light. The overhead lighting is dim and candles glow everywhere, the light soft, the air still, silent. I notice a Bible and some books on a small table in the front of the church. I think, *I'll just read* and settle into a pew. Suddenly, I'm not sitting on a hard pew. I'm in some other space, a place where I have never been before. It glows, shimmers. I'm suddenly wrapped and pulled into a Presence. It feels as though the whole church is now filled with this Presence. I'm held by a golden, shimmering light. I am with Him. I am aware it is Christ. I don't know how I know. I just know. I wonder if I'm supposed to say something and then I know inside I only need to be with Him. I don't see Him like I'd see someone on a subway. I see Him with eyes that are different, my inside eyes. A man in a glowing robe, bearded, tired, a bit stooped, a man who is the focus. I move into some intimate communion with him. It seems like I feel what he is feeling. Pain and then great compassion. He knows what is coming. I see it in his face, accepting, waiting. I have no idea how long I sit there. I'm not afraid. I feel the glow and shimmer of the space enter me. He never looks at me, but I know He knows I'm there. I know that's all He needs. We sit together, present with each other.

My father appears and I'm startled back into the church with a thump, surprised that an hour has passed. We drive home in quiet. My father is not a small-talk person. I tell him it was an amazing experience. I know he hears me, but he doesn't respond as is his manner. When we get home, I go straight to bed, still filled with the power of that Presence. I feel it in every cell of me, liquid gold.

From that very first experience as a fifteen-year-old, I have found my life to be awash with many such experiences. Some of great import and some like quicksilver, some subtle. Each one came to me unexpectedly, unbidden, given.

For a few years, off and on, I think seriously about entering a convent. The thought of a cloistered life appeals to me.

Hours spent in meditation, in ritual, in service, in peace and contemplation. I explore some possibilities. But over time, the thoughts of such a life begin to fade. It would be another forty years before I again experienced such a powerful event in a church. But there were other paths that appeared that led into this world I came to experience as mystical.

There is a music inside me. I feel it. Always there, sometimes distant, sometimes so close like a brook, murmuring. The music comes in different forms. Sometimes it is in images, colors, light and dark, shadows, dreams. Piano keys— parallel sounds, meanings. Am I the only one who hears?

Curiosity was an element in my universe. Something as basic as the earth, always there. I probably tasted the fluid in the birth canal on my way out, thinking, *how interesting*. Someone once asked me about my earliest memory, and this is what flowed. A memory of color and shape and a density of space that fills an undefined time. I have memory of a time before I had words. The color is dark, a dark reddish brown, like a mixture of burnt sienna and burnt umber with shifting waves of cadmium orange and viridian playing around the edges like northern lights, a glimmer but not enough to bring light into the center. The color has shape and density and texture. It is round and soft and fills all space. It is warm. It encircles without having edges. It has a weight that is not heavy but is enough to hold the mass around me. The sound is no sound. I feel as though it travels with me through all the time for which I do not yet have thoughts that can become words. A dark, formless space where I live until I can speak

As a child, I could not have articulated any of this. All I knew was a world with a warm and loving grandmother and moody, distant parents. I was alone a lot. My sister was born four and a half years later, too much of a gap in time to support friendship. That happened in adulthood. I did what I think most children do. I invented friends to play with. I incorporated animals into my life as friends. I invented my own world.

I walk up the alley behind our house on my way to school, passing some garages with wooden doors painted gray and a few row homes on the left. On the right is the silk mill. Colors of that alley were gray, dirty white, and the brick-red of the mill. I come to the cement steps on the left that take me up to Gordon Street. I cross that street to a narrow walkway in between rows of houses. In my mind, I name that alley Spike Alley because a big brown boxer lives there behind a chain-link fence. I see his name on his collar. Every time I pass, I call his name. He is a friend on my way to school.

When I leave Spike Alley, in my mind I ride my horse. My horse doesn't have a name, but I gallop him along the streets until I come to a big yard with a wide-swinging metal gate. By then my horse is tired and I dismount, open the gate, lead him in, and get a fresh horse out of the yard. I'm always careful to close the gate and wonder if the people who live there watch me do this. Then I ride the rest of the way to school. My animal friends are always there when I need them.

I have Tinker Toys, Lincoln Logs, and a whole plastic farm with a barn and fences and trees and animals, especially horses. I love horses. I ride them into my imagination, my dreams and give them names and family histories and record all their names, which come from Greek mythology, in a notebook. I don't know how I know those names. I read a lot, maybe that's how I know them. My father gives me an old alarm clock, and I love taking it all apart to see how it works and then I put it all together to do again another day.

I don't remember ever feeling lonely. I had a few neighborhood friends, my animals, and the ever-changing world of nature. And I had my imagination. These were the places I disappeared into when my parents moved in and out of their moods. In later years, I came to understand that my mother was chronically depressed, and I finally could name what it was that I felt from her. My father probably was too. And so, I played in my mind.

I was anchored as a child by the Lutheran church and our immigrant neighborhood and community. I just followed the norms of that culture. Weekly Sunday school, Saturday school for a while, which included German language instruction, junior choir, Luther League, a teen group, and church picnics. Outside of these forms, I lived in relation to the outdoors, walks in the woods with my dog along the Jordan River that ran by our house, and finding my survival places living with depressed parents. All shaped my internal landscape.

Thinking back now, I hear the beginnings of melodies that became part of me. It was the music of my ancestors' world: church music, hymns that were part of both Austrian and German cultures. They still wrap around me. The sounds of Bach, Brahms, Martin Luther, Handel, Schumann, Mendelssohn, and Wagner filled my church life as well as my home, as my mother loved classical music and played it often on her mahogany-red RCA phonograph. Through all these years, the sounds of the natural world also became part of me. I would walk alone in the woods by the time I was eight. I loved doing that. I entered that world and learned the sounds, the rich smell of the earth, the colors of birds, insects, the wind, the cool shade of trees, the rush of the stream when it was high with spring melt and the gurgles when it was low in late summer. The sounds made their own symphony and entered my being as accompaniment to hymns.

There was one other German composer, Hildegard von Bingen, who lived five centuries earlier than the ones I knew from my growing up, but I did not find her until decades later. Her music led me to another world that was both old and new.

Other bits of melody begin to build. Uncle Oscar, my bachelor uncle who lives up the street with Nanny, belongs to the Liederkranz, a club supporting German culture. It is only a fifteen-minute walk away, and he stops by our house to collect us on nights when his men's singing group has concerts there. The singers always feature German folk songs and romantic ditties and wear red vests to liven things up. In addition, our family and many others often gather at the club on Saturday nights when an oompah band plays mostly polkas and waltzes. The band members, in their lederhosen, play with gusto. The tuba, drums, accordion, trumpet, clarinet, and trombone bring everyone out on the dance floor at some point. People, young and old, whirl around, laughing, cheeks rosy. Beer, soft drinks, cheese, ring baloney, and giant pretzels are served at tables surrounding the dance floor. Joyful memories of music binding community. My foot still taps as I think of those days.

It is a bright, sunny morning in late winter, with the air carrying a hint of spring. My mind on this quiet morning walk plays with thoughts generated by some readings I've recently discovered about mystics throughout church history. Sometimes I believe I was born into that group, although I had no inkling when I was a child. I have been drawn by them for as long as I can remember. They have flowed in and out of my life, through writings appearing on bookshelves or at conferences, finding their way into my hands and life.

In an online search for information about mystics, I located Fr. Ronald Rolheiser, OMI. He is the past president of the Oblate School of Theology in San Antonio, Texas. One of his talks stays with me, powerfully. It was a presentation on mystics among other topics, but toward the end, he commented on how our contemporary world does not support the spiritual path of people in the final years of their lives. He calls this period the time of letting go, the time of giving attention to and preparing for the final transition from this world. Because of my years of working in health care, often with aging populations, I called Fr. Rolheiser, telling him of my interest in this area and asked for suggestions for further reading. He recommended *The Gift of Peace*, by Joseph Cardinal Bernardin. It is the cardinal's personal reflection of his path through pancreatic cancer. He came to see death as a friend rather than an enemy. Close to the end of his life, he wrote about the need to let go of what we no longer need to make room for God to work within us. Fr. Rolheiser also talked about several other mystics, one of whom was Hildegard von Bingen, a nun who lived in the early Middle Ages. I looked her up and found well-researched material about her life.

I connected with this mystic. I felt an affinity, a kinship with her.

Hildegard was born in 1098 in Germany. As a child, she began to experience visions, which lasted throughout her life. She was sent to a Benedictine monastery at about nine years of age and lived in that community until her death at eighty-one, one year older than I am as I write. In a male-dominated medieval society, she was a woman ahead of her time. She was a poet, a visionary, a musician, a healer using the gifts of plants, an advocate for peace, and eventually an abbess of her own convent. I share with her the experiences of what I now call mystical, which I have had most of my life, my loving intention to heal, and a need to write.

Now I remember a book tucked away among many on one of my bookshelves. Several years ago, I co-authored a chapter titled "Spirituality and Aging" for the textbook, *Occupational Therapy with Aging Adults*. I sit down and read what I wrote. What I see is that I know! I know how to connect and guide people through this part of their lives. I know how to connect with their spirit, with their innermost vulnerable places. Their innermost places of both pain and hope. I know how to guide them, often to a place of peace. I still know how to do this. It's part of me.

A case study I wrote for this book is as follows:

"Thomas Johnson," a seventy-four-year-old African American gentleman, was admitted to the gerontological unit I was working on in a large, mid-South hospital system. He was terminally ill with cancer. His wife requested that he be referred for rehabilitation if possible because she wished to be able to take him home so he could die there. He was a retired president of a church-affiliated university in that community and was loved and respected for his leadership and commitment. Both occupational and physical therapy were ordered.

When I walked into his room, I was shocked at his condition. He was a tall man but was frail and very wasted.

"Hello Mr. Johnson," I said quietly, touching his hand, which lay flat on the white sheet. My touch was as gentle as my voice. First communications: voice and touch. "My name is Judy. I'll be helping to see if we can find ways to improve your strength so your wife will be able to support you more effectively at home." I neither felt nor saw any response to my words.

His eyes were open, but I could not find a place in them to connect with him. He was alive, but there was no life in him. The feeling I had was that he had given up and was no longer engaged with life. I felt strongly that my first goal needed to be to awaken his spirit, to find a spark of connection.

His wife was a gentle presence and her love for and pride in her husband were palpable. I came to feel she was part of the treatment team, even though she generally just sat quietly in the room.

Addressing them both I asked, "What kind of activity would be most meaningful, a place to begin?"

"The first thing he does every morning is shave. I think that would be a good place to start," she said.

"I agree with you," I said. Mr. Johnson did not respond even though the question was addressed to him as well.

Treatment sessions lasted only ten to fifteen minutes because of his weakness. I came twice a day. That was all he could tolerate. We used his electric razor, and in the beginning, he could neither grip nor hold it. I fitted him with a universal cuff, a plastic device designed to hold the razor and that wrapped around his palm. I wrapped my hand around his, and we began to shave him. As the days went on, he became able to hold the razor and partially shave the side of his face. I finished the rest. Bit by bit, he began to manage more of the task himself and at discharge, he was able to shave himself totally.

The activity was never the goal. It was the means for him to re-engage with life. We did not talk a lot. His level of endurance would not allow this. But I grew to know him well. I always entered his room with the belief that he was alive and well and whole in spirit. I saw him that way. Progress was incremental. First, he began to make eye contact with me. Then I saw the hint of a smile. Then I saw life begin to appear in his eyes and we began to enjoy the interchange of eye contact and smiles. I felt that I had entered his space. It was a time we could share as was the time I shared with Christ as a fifteen-year-old. I touched him every day and in my touch was the intention to heal, deliberate. My time of knowing Mr. Johnson felt sacred.

All of us knew he probably would not shave himself at home, at least not for long. They would have help, and his wife was devoted and loving. But when he left, he was a person who was living.

That evening I prepared a simple meal, tired but grateful for the experience of knowing this man and his wife. We gave something to each other, a reason for being. After dinner, I turned on one of my favorite recordings of Hildegard von Bingen and allowed myself to rest. The soaring melody of her became my rhythm, allowing me healing and peace.

This was another case study I contributed for the same textbook:

I took communion (as a volunteer layperson) to a woman in our church community who was hospitalized with metastatic breast cancer. Norma was elderly and had spent her entire work life as a teacher's aide. After completing the communion process, I asked her how she felt. She said, "I am afraid." I asked her if she was afraid of dying. She said, "Yes, but I've got to fight. I thought I was dying the other night." Then she looked at me and said, "There is no caring in this place." Her room was right across from the nurse's station, and I saw people in white moving busily and hurriedly around in that space, but no one investigated her room.

Norma rarely reclined anymore because of difficulty breathing, so she was propped up in a sitting position with an assortment of pillows.

"Sometimes at night some of the staff let me rest my head on their stomach for a minute," she said.

"Would you like me to hold you?" I asked.

"Yes," she said.

I got up, reached around her, and held her. She held on to my arm and after a few minutes, she let go, saying that was enough. She said, "It helps calm me to be held and I am OK now." She died three days later.

I thought that evening, it took so little to hear her need and meet it, the need for human touch and connection in a time of fear and vulnerability. A healing connection in a place that could not heal her body.

How? How did I arrive at this place of being able to hear and love and support? What was my path from the child, the dreamer, into a world that is sometimes beyond this world, into spaces and places that cannot be quantified?

I am an ordinary woman in some space and time. I pull out my favorite CD of Hildegard von Bingen. The music wraps around me, a gentle blessing as I write. Women's voices joined in unison soar effortlessly through octaves of amazing range. Pure melody washes over me, glittering gold-and-silver waves rising and falling, taking me into a place of spirit. The beauty of it stays with me, becomes a rhythm in me as I move through my days. I am filled with the same glow and shimmering light that I experienced in the church at fifteen.

Hildegard's music is rooted in Gregorian chant but is significantly more expressive than the three-to-four-note range of that form of music. She thought that liturgy should be beautiful, with lines of melody leaping up and flowing down. She also set her poetry to music. There is something in her musical expression that touches me, that makes me feel joyous and flowing but also opens in me a space to feel things unsaid. Murmurs of the soul. This is my thread.

Fifty years later, on a day of reflection, I was brought back to an Easter season in which my husband slipped away as I lay beside him on the hospital bed. It had been a long illness, hard on us both. He was ready to go. I remember that I had to consciously and deliberately push through something deep inside me to let him go. Finally, he just stopped breathing. In the moment of his dying, I felt that space, that space of such love and intimacy, much deeper than the time of living. The passing was an immeasurable moment of time, but was a tangible event like the flutter of a butterfly wing. I then remember my time in the church that Maundy Thursday and the closeness I felt with Christ as he drew closer to his death. There was no sense of conventional time then either, but there was that same sense of closeness and love much deeper than the time of living.

One year later, almost to the day, my mother died. She was eighty-nine, and we had had time for closure on all kinds of levels. We had time also to just be with each other without needing to talk. She was in hospice care and she and I and my sister knew the reality. We were with her, each holding one of her hands. At her last breath, she sat up and looked straight ahead as though seeing someone or something that held her gaze. And then, in that immeasurable moment of time, she was gone. In my reflection, the feeling of her moment of death was also like my moment in the presence of Christ, a place without any conventional meaning of time. A place, a space that existed on some other plane.

Today, there is a light snow but no wind. A lovely day for a walk with my favorite classical music still in my mind from the radio earlier this morning. It was my mother who brought that music to me. I was moved even as a young child by the classical composers she favored.

Memories of these melodies carry me not back but forward, the energy a vehicle for new thoughts.

My parents, forever marked by the Great Depression, grew up in a world still tied to gender-defined roles, as well as the traditions of the church and the old-world norms brought by their parents, my grandparents, from Austria.

Always curious about people and growing up in an immigrant community, I was aware of different languages, foods, smells, ways of laughing, ways of arguing. I lived in a cultural stew and enjoyed it all. My mother must have seen something about that in me because when I was nine or ten, she got me a subscription to *Natural History Magazine*. I could not wait for the monthly issues to arrive and looked first for the articles about different cultures and then for different ways of healing. The wanting to know about healing was there at nine or ten. I think perhaps it was there from the beginning and grew out of love. Love for all living creatures.

It was also about this time that I found a magazine on a store shelf that caught my eye. It was *Arizona Highways*. I saved my allowance and sent for a subscription. The photographs of the landscape, the colors, the stark beauty connected me immediately to the books that I found on my Uncle Oscar's bookshelf, written by Zane Grey. That author's novels were most often set in Arizona. And so started my lifelong love affair with the Southwest. What I found as I learned more about the native peoples of that area during the time I lived there later in my life were values based on respect, a reverence for the land, and a spiritual life that grew from the earth, the sky, its seasons, and its wonders.

In *Sacred Earth, Sacred Soul, Celtic Wisdom for Reawakening to What Our Souls Know and Healing the Earth*, John Philip Newell explores the nature of Celtic spirituality from its origins. I became interested in his writing and discovered similarity with the values I found in the Southwest. He describes the foundation of Celtic wisdom as being one of holding everything on our planet as sacred, including the planet itself, all living creatures, every stone, ripple of water, cloud, animal, and human. When I read the phrase, "what our souls know," I knew. I occupy a space where my soul knows.

It is Newell's premise that in an increasingly technological world, we have lost that connection with the sacred. But for me, vestiges linger. I remember one sunny, warm day in my years living in the Rio Grande Valley. I am in the yard and am drawn to the brilliant red hibiscus that I had planted at the corner of my healing room. It grows well there, and I walk over to admire it as I do every day. There on one of the leaves is a green anole, a small lizard native to warm climates, perhaps five inches long. It is still, quiet. I very slowly move my index finger toward it, hoping to touch it. The anole then slowly stretches a pale green front foot toward my finger, reaching with five toes fanned out, a bit sticky on the ends, and touches it. We both stay still for a moment. I cannot forget the soft, careful, delicate touch, testing, trusting. I can feel it as I write. A sacred moment.

My growing-up world was predictable. Family and church were the centers. My father talked about sports, my mother talked about how none of the ministers we ever had were any good, and later about all the politics behind the scenes at the college she worked at by then, and where my sister and I went because we got free tuition. Uncle Oscar talked incessantly about the history of the Austro-Hungarian empire. The themes were like repeated melodies, heard so often they become background noise. But then, a different kind of person appeared who changed the shape of my thinking. He brought a new melody.

Dr. Hagen Staack was a Lutheran pastor who emigrated to Allentown after the war. He became our minister and guided our congregation for five years. He was the one and only minister my mother ever approved of. Her reasons?

"He is really from Germany, so he speaks excellent German and he's on time for everything." What I saw, as a pre-teen and then teen, over those five years was someone who showed her a different world.

Hagen Staack did his religious training as part of the Confessing Church in Nazi Germany. During the years 1935-1939, Dietrich Bonhoeffer illegally trained seminarians for the ministry in the Confessing Church. Students had to have a cover for being accepted at the university and Dr. Staack enrolled with a major in geology. After completing this degree, he served in the German army as a chaplain, was injured, and served time in a Russian prison camp. He loved preaching and teaching and enjoyed people. His mind was always active, searching, learning. A man different from my father.

Staack asked my mother to help edit a book he was writing. She spoke fluent German, which was her first language, and loved to write herself. She was the church secretary at the time, and she took on this task with eagerness. They worked together at the church for those five years, and he provided our whole family with a window into something new. We became close with his wife and children, and he was often in our home working on the book with my mother. He spent time with my sister and me as well, often talking about geology, fossils, and the structure of the earth. He talked to me about archaeology and became a mentor and a teacher about life paths that I had not thought of. My mind opened to new mysteries, new cultures, new concepts of time. Was this another stream that nourished my wish to learn and experience times and spaces different than mine? When his five years were over, he took a position as the head of the Religion Department at Muhlenberg College in Allentown and told my mother about a position as secretary for the Department of Education. She applied, got the job, and her world changed, as did ours.

What was it, I wonder, about those years that were underpinnings of my sense of myself now, as mystic, healer, and seeker of a contemplative way of being? The years from pre-teen through college and finally leaving home were turbulent for me. There is nothing new about growing pains and conflict in families, especially during years of change. I can see now how difficult it must have been for my mother, who wanted my sister and me to have a better life and more opportunity than she did and felt that she was the only one responsible to make that happen. If I were to paint a picture of her at that time, it would be of a woman standing over me wringing her hands, with a look of total frustration.

"Judy," she said, her voice tight. "You come home and read books that don't have anything to do with your coursework. And then you don't start studying until late at night. Don't you know that college is work?"

I heard that more than once. "I know, Mom. I'll do better."

I did not have the wisdom or words in those years to express what I needed. I also knew that if I did have the words, she would not be able to understand.

The protected place in me grew larger.

When I started high school, my father created a room for me in the attic that was just mine. Until then, I did have my own room on the second floor, but the only bathroom in the house was off my bedroom, so everyone walked through my bedroom to bathe or use the bathroom. That attic room became my contemplative space, my cell. I painted it lavender and bought lavender sheets for my bed. No one came up there except occasionally an invited friend.

I survived those years because I had that space and I had nature and I had my imagination. I could not study until everyone else in the house was asleep, and all was quiet, with no distractions. In the house without adequate insulation, I heard everything. I was taking art classes on and off, and it was in that room that I sketched and drew and painted. One of the pieces of work was published in the college arts magazine. It was also in that room that I started writing little stories, one of which was also published in the same magazine. It was about a small spider that appeared almost nightly at my desk, which my father had built into my dormer window. I think it may have been the warmth of the lamp that drew him out. I named him Petey, and he became a friend. I would chat with him and then I imagined a whole world around him and his spider family and wrote about it. Interestingly, about five years later, I married my first husband whose name was Pete. It was also in that room where I began journaling, which I still do. There were two dormer windows, one facing east across the railroad tracks, the Jordan River, and the factories on the other side. The other faced west, and I could look out at the homes built up the side of the hill behind our house like so many small boulders piled on one another. I could just sit quietly and look out of those windows and travel to another place.

It was also a room where I could be in quiet, in peace. I see, and know now, that I have always needed time to be quiet and away. Perhaps that was as much a part of my being as was curiosity and the love of the earth and the natural world. In that way, I did not fit into my family of origin. They did not understand my need to be still, my need to be quiet. The work ethic was so strongly impressed on my mother that she felt that everyone, including me, should feel the same way, and if I did not fall into line, she let me know I was falling short. In some similar ways, I still do not fit in the world in which I live. I have always followed my own path. My mother, I think, never understood my wish to leave my hometown or to choose to stay in many jobs for only about two years, leaving when I needed more growth or new challenges. She accepted my divorce, but I think did not fully understand. The difference now is that I know that is my path, always curious, always needful of quiet contemplative time, always a seeker.

I sit in quiet today, having a need to step back, to reflect. Suddenly I come face to face with a truth that I did not see as a child. I wrote about my plastic farm with families of horses, all identified, all knowing each other, built from a gift I received when I was about eleven or twelve. And then I wrote about a spider that came to be my study companion and built for him a story about his big family. Suddenly, I knew that my young self was creating in her imagination a family that she wished she had, a house filled with warmth and love and many beings that lived in community. I fall off a ledge into a deep sadness and, then more clearly, a sadness for that young person who had to find a way to create for herself what was not available to her in her family of origin. The sadness stays with me for most of the day, but then I begin to think that perhaps I am being taught, by my imagination, by animals, by nature, and by guides in my life who appear at significant times. And I finally think that the images I created in my early years may be what has strengthened and supported me through hard times and hopefully has allowed me to provide for my daughters and grandchildren what I did not have.

During those years, other issues were tugging at me as I think is true of most young people in their late teens. I took two religion courses in college, taught by Dr. Hagen Staack: The History of Religion and History of the Jewish People. My reasons for enrolling in these two courses were several. I knew this man was an excellent teacher. His thoughts and flow of information were clear and concise. In addition, I just wanted to know more, always more about the shape and texture of religious experience over centuries. I was not thinking about visions as I had not yet identified events that appeared unbidden and from a different plane. I just wanted to know about how our Western view of God was similar or different from that of other cultures and centuries. Looking back, I can say I have always been a seeker. I joined a small study group that met to study Hebrew. My major was classical languages and there were only seven of us in the whole college with that major. The other six were students who became Lutheran ministers. My intent was to be an archaeologist, influenced in some part by Dr. Staack and in some part by my imaginative dreams of going off to exotic lands and digging in the dirt to find glorious relics. By my junior year, I knew that was no longer my path, but what to do?

I had been taking all the art courses I could fit into my schedule with an instructor named Al Colarusso. He was the only art instructor on campus and was a good teacher who enjoyed what he did and enjoyed the students. I talked with him about my lack of focus on what I would do after graduation. I mentioned looking for an MFA program. This was his response:

"I would be glad to help you develop a portfolio if you would like to apply to an MFA program, but why don't you take a year and just work?" He must have seen the shocked look on my face because he followed this with, "It seems like a long time, but it's just a drop in the bucket of life." This advice was one of the most important turning points in my life.

The Allentown State Hospital in those days housed about 3,000 chronically mentally ill people. I found a job there as an activity instructor for about sixty chronic schizophrenic men. I would continue to live at home, develop a plan to save money, and embark on something new.

New it was. I was young, with no experience in health care or in mental health. I did experience a summer traveling in Europe, connecting first with an ecumenical student group in Bavaria, then a trip to East Berlin, and ending in southeastern Austria with the opportunity to visit relatives. Despite these experiences, I was a blank slate. I had a supervisor, Miyeko Harada, who was the occupational therapist for the institution. She was a good and caring teacher and taught me a great deal about that population as well as about occupational therapy. This was to be a summer job, but I ended up working there for eighteen months. I loved the new learning. The hospital had a fine library, and that's where I went in my spare time to read everything I could about psychiatric care and diagnoses. I came to love the patients. I didn't know what to expect. Many of these men, all dressed in khaki work slacks, blue shirts, and brown shoes, were either nonverbal or talked to people I could not see. But a number were friendly, sometimes conversant, and asked questions about their projects and wanted to please, to do well. What filled me was the mystery of the human brain. I lived with that mystery for those eighteen months, trying to learn but mostly interacting, observing, and learning from the patients. They all communicated but in ways that would not have fit outside of the hospital. They expressed their needs in facial expression or non-expression in language that was their own. I learned to listen to more than words.

An author I came across just a few years ago, Richard Wagamese, was an Ojibwe from northwestern Ontario. Before he died in 2017, he received recognition and acclaim for his writing in Canada and beyond. *Embers* was one of his sixteen books and is a collection of his meditations. This one spoke to me:

> *I used to believe my body contained my soul ... I came to believe that it's the other way around. My soul contains my body. It is everything that I am. I am never separate from Creator except for in my mind. ... I know the truth of what my people say: that we are all spirit, we are all energy, joined to everything that is everywhere, all things coming true together.*

Wagamese articulated what I could not. In my early twenties, my life experience was limited, except for that summer spent in Europe. My mother was a secretary and my father a steelworker. Their parents were struggling immigrants trying to understand the new world they moved into. My father did not believe children should see their parents argue, so my sister and I never saw them arguing. It was not a question-asking world. We just did what we had to do or were told to do, and questioning was never encouraged. I am not sure I ever thought about the concept of soul except for what was talked about in sermons or Bible readings. But I did have a belief, I think almost before I could form sentences, that there was something within people and animals and plants and trees and the wind that I could communicate with and that I wanted to communicate with. Words were not necessary. When I read Wagamese's poem I heard myself talking. My time working at the Allentown State Hospital, I believe, was the beginning of my understanding of how to see a person's soul.

My experience at the state hospital led me to a career that lasted for forty-two years. Miyeko—or Eko as she preferred to be called—spent a lot of time teaching me about occupational therapy. She made sure I had a wide variety of experiences and encouraged me to think about OT as a career. She supported me in finding funding and helped with my application to Columbia University College of Physicians and Surgeons in New York. I was accepted, and I quickly said yes. Then I told my parents. My decision was hardest on my mother. She clearly wanted me to stay home and become a part of the population that lived and spent their lives in the same place, to be her friend. I saw her disappointment.

"Mom, New York is just a two-hour bus ride away. I can come home often on weekends, but I have to go." My parents became quiet. I felt their sadness, but they offered no argument.

I loved living in my rented room in New York. The city was so alive. I was comfortable with the mix of cultures, smells, colors, and sounds that changed every few city blocks. I was excited about my new learning, the studies, my new friends. But after a few months, I felt a need for a quiet space. I hadn't yet been able to find that in the city. So, I went home for a weekend. Everyone was clearly glad to see me, and it felt good to be there. I asked my parents if I could borrow their car for an afternoon, and they agreed willingly.

The next afternoon, I drove out into the countryside surrounding Allentown. The weather was still warm. I had no clear idea about where I wanted to go. I just knew I needed quiet, peace, space. I drove for a while through rolling hills of farmland and came to a gentle valley with fields on both sides of the road, some with newly harvested corn or wheat, some fallow. I saw a place where I could pull over safely, stopped the car, got out, and walked over to the wood rail fence surrounding a wide, green pasture. There were no animals or people about.

I know this is the place I need to be, a quiet space to rest. How deeply I need nature and space and time away from the frantic pace of the city. I climb over the fence and walk up the gentle slope, stopping about halfway. I still see no sign of people or livestock, so I find a level, grassy area and lie down on my back. The sky is a clear, cerulean blue with occasional wisps of white clouds floating without form or direction. The sun is warm, and I let myself relax into its golden glow. I smell the earth, hear insects and birds in a nearby tree. A faint breeze soothes my skin, my mind clears.

Suddenly I am part of the field. My spine feels like it is sinking into the earth and becomes part of it, stretching, easing. Slowly, my arms and legs begin to stretch. I feel them begin to reach and move to the far corners of the pasture, coming close to the fence. Now I am part of the planet, and I feel the earth's rotation in space. It is a most amazing feeling. It feels like something beyond, that I always wanted to touch. I lay in that time and space until I felt something walking across my cheek. I reach up and startle a grasshopper. Then I turn my head and see that the sun is close to the horizon. My body is quickly moving back to its original form, allowing me to sit up and understand that it is time to go home. As I drive, I suddenly remember that this experience of feeling in a different world space and place was like the feeling I had in the church when I was fifteen, when I was suddenly in a space where I had never been before, enveloped by it.

My years in New York were very busy with the occupational therapy program. My schedule was packed, sometimes up to twenty credit hours a semester, with classes on three different campuses throughout the city. Subject matter was all new to me, comprising gross anatomy, physiology, neuroanatomy, orthopedics, medicine and surgery, and psychology. Added in were labs that applied all this new learning to crafts and how to use them, along with what we were learning in formal classwork, to treat clients. Integration of all this material took up almost all my time, and I wondered how I would ever find that kind of peaceful nourishment in my busy life in a busy city.

But I did discover that tickets, in those days still afford-able for students, were available for performances at Lincoln Center. It was here that I found the space that fed my soul with music. There was one special performance of the New York Philharmonic which is still clear in my mind. Leonard Bernstein was conducting. At the beginning of the second half of the evening, he came out on stage and announced a special guest. The spotlight followed his hand as he lifted it toward a red velvet-draped box on the right, high up toward the ceiling. An elderly man with snow-white hair slowly stood and bowed to the audience.

"Please meet Igor Stravinsky," Bernstein said, "the com-poser of the piece we are about to play for you, *The Rite of Spring.*" The applause from the audience lasted for a long time before the music finally began, transporting me to a place deep inside. On another evening, at the New York City Ballet, the featured piece was *Romeo and Juliet*. The principal dancers for that performance were Rudolf Nureyev and Dame Margot Fonteyn. Their connection was intimate, strong, pure grace, and totally wrapped in the music. I felt as though I was seeing the face of God.

In addition to Lincoln Center, I sometimes walked over to the west side of Manhattan and walked along the Hudson River, where I could feel space, see seabirds, and hear river traffic. Once in a great while, I took the Staten Island Ferry over and back, just to get out on water, feel the breeze, and be among a new group of people. Later, Washington Square Park became one of my favorite places to just sit and people-watch.

Two other places of nourishment remain in my mem-ory. One was a Lutheran church I found on the lower end of Manhattan. I dropped in one Sunday and discovered that this church was home for people in the arts: the theater, orches-tras, art centers, poets, musicians. They came dressed in what-ever felt right to them and none would have fit into the con-gregation of St. Peter's in Allentown. It was refreshing and joyful in feeling. The pastor did wear his white clerical collar and black shirt but was clearly happy in his role of ministering to this group. The other place was a large auditorium in central Manhattan. I no longer remember the name, but every spring, advertisements went out inviting all who were interested to come and sing Handel's *Messiah*. Rehearsals were held weekly and on Easter, the group, which numbered in the hundreds, performed this beautiful piece of music. One of my OT classmates had a wonderful voice and urged me to come with her. I did not have a wonderful voice, but it didn't matter. It was one of the most spiritual moments of my time there. A time when I was enfolded in the music, the soaring melody.

Elements of my classes taught me in a way that had nothing to do with facts. In one of the labs, we were learning how to do components of a test that was non-verbal in nature for use with psychiatric patients. There were four or five art activities involved, one of which was creating some sort of sculpture out of a ball of clay. I was comfortable with this as I had done similar things with my patients at the state hospital. What emerged from my ball of gray clay was a figure holding out its hands. When I looked at what I created, I suddenly circled the sculpture with my arms, protecting what I had done. What it was to me was myself, holding out my hands, asking. I felt very vulnerable. I stayed in that position for a while, wondering at how strong that feeling was. I was experiencing the power of nonverbal expression with media. I carried that lesson with me for all my career. Now, thinking back, I connect that moment with a time in which I still had not shared my unusual experiences with anyone. I had yet to name them as mystical.

After I had processed my new learning and began practicing, I was met daily with opportunities to witness the courage, adaptability, pain, and suffering, as well as the amazing strength of the people who came to be in my care. Faced with life-changing injury or illness, they worked, struggled, chose to live, and became my teachers. I learned to find their souls. For me, the path to healing always begins there.

Pete and I were married in 1968. We were twenty-six. I wanted children very much and after a year we started trying. The years went by. Frustrating years. I sometimes burst into tears when pregnant women walked by me on the street. We found an OB/GYN that we both liked and began a long series of fertility tests, none of which were conclusive, none of which showed a fixable reason as to why we couldn't get pregnant. We began an adoption process and after nine months, our daughter Mary arrived. She was two-and-a-half when she came, and I was three months pregnant with our second child. They say it happens that way sometimes. Our second daughter, Katie, was born in December, six months later by emergency Caesarean section. It was a challenging time. Happy and joyous, but financially difficult as I had stopped work when Mary arrived. But we bit the bullet. I continued to stay home with my two babies.

All of this happened in the early '70s. Governmental fiscal policies impacted the nation and the inflationary spiral began. Our financial situation was pinched. We had a mortgage and one car and began juggling our bills. I sometimes sat looking around our house to see if there was anything we could sell: paintings on the wall, furniture, or utensils we didn't need.

Four months after my second daughter was born, I had an IUD inserted. One day in May, I learned I was pregnant again. I was shaken but also excited. I had always imagined having more children. I dearly loved the two we already had. When my husband came home from work, I sat down with him and told him, still feeling my excitement but unsure about his reaction.

He didn't move but his face did. He looked shocked and

didn't speak for a minute. Then he said, "We can't have it."

"What?" I said, disbelieving.

He said again, "We can't have it. I don't know if I could support us."

I felt torn up inside and started to argue, quietly. I said, "I can go back to work, and we can put the children in day care, and we would do all right financially." In my mind, I knew that we could do it.

He repeated, "We can't have it," and got up and walked away. What I was left with was my despair but also the sound of my husband's voice. I had never heard that tone before. Almost as though he was close to walking off his own cliff.

I was a health-care professional. I knew the timeline was very short. Within a few days, I was in my doctor's office asking for a D&C. "My husband does not want this," I told him. It was painful. This man had worked long and patiently to try and find a way for us to be pregnant. He was excited for us when our daughter was born. I saw his face, probably mirroring mine, but he made no judgment.

One day soon after, I got up early, took my children to their sitter's house, and told them I would be back to get them in the morning. My husband had told me he had a business conference he had to be at in another city, so he could not be with me.

When I was being wheeled into the OR on the gurney, all I heard was my head screaming, "No, No, No." I stayed overnight and before I left in the morning, the doctor came in and told me they discovered the IUD had migrated into my uterine wall. The explanation for the pregnancy.

When my husband came home later that night, he said, "Is it done?"

I said, "Yes."

That was the last time we talked about the event until four years later when we finalized our divorce. I told him then the only thing I regretted in our eleven years together was the abortion.

He said, "I don't know why I did that."

I was depressed for most of the year following the abortion. What kept me even and functioning were my children. My bedrock of normalcy. I was angry at my husband for years and years, and I was unforgiving of myself. Why did I allow this? The act went against everything in my being. It was a spiritual loss. The loss of a child which I allowed.

As days and then weeks passed, I began to feel the presence of that child. It was a boy. I knew. His spirit stayed with me, connected, a light shining in my heart. I named him Benjamin. He is still part of me.

Sometime after we moved to Memphis, Tennessee, and after the divorce, I went to church one morning as was my pattern.

I sit quietly. The sermon goes on and I listen but am not really hearing. Just sitting. Suddenly a strong beam of golden light from the cross on the altar shines on me. It's a broad beam and very bright. I look around at the other people to see if it's shining on them and if they notice. I look back at the cross, thinking it must be a figment of my imagination, but the golden light is still there and shining only on me. No one else seems to notice. I just sit. After several minutes, it's suddenly gone. I look around again to see if there is some light fixture in the church that might be reflected from the cross or a beam of light from the window that might have glanced off it. There is nothing. I just sit, wondering, and then I know. I know within that directed, golden light that I was forgiven. Forgiven by that compassionate man I had first met when I was fifteen. A man who understood pain and suffering yet continued his path. And so, I continued mine, but it would take many, many more years for me to understand and accept that I could forgive myself and step out of my cage of self-recrimination.

Decades later, I finally understood that I had created the box to house my pain and chose to live in it. After discussion with a few close friends, I decided to share with my daughters what had happened. I wanted to tell them why for many years, off and on, they lived with a mother who kept bumping into her own anger and guilt, which I knew sometimes spilled out into their lives. They were now adults with families of their own. My older daughter's reaction was immediate. She said, "That's when your marriage ended."

My younger daughter had two responses. "It was a boy," she said.

"Yes," I said.

Then she said, "You were so alone," and wept. They were supportive of both me and their father and made no judgment.

Another decade passed, and I finally understood my husband's response. His reaction I believe was about survival. Influenced by the values he grew up with which were about the man's ability to provide for and be the head of the family, I remembered his words. "I don't know if I could support us." My pain was spiritual. I made a choice to say goodbye to a child I truly wanted. It took me a long time to forgive myself, to find compassion for myself, understanding all the forces that were acting on us.

Pain and loss come to all of us at some point in our lives. I didn't realize it then, but this dark time allowed me to later understand levels of loss and pain that my patients experienced. I also now know, within minutes sometimes, if a person I meet is also locked in a self-created box of guilt and pain. Knowing that, I know how to meet them, how to support and guide them, and sometimes lead them to self-awareness and peace.

In his book, *The Wounded Healer*, Henri Nouwen shares his premise that the healing ministry takes away the illusion that wholeness can be given by one to another. It is healing because it sees the loneliness and the pain of another, inviting him to recognize his loneliness in a way that can be shared. In other words, we are all wounded. If we enter our own woundedness with awareness, we can then enter the woundedness of others. Rachel Naomi Remen writes that healing is a matter of wisdom, not of science. In an article from *Noetic Sciences Review*, spring of 1996 titled "In the Service of Life," she offers that when we serve others, we serve from ourselves, from all our experiences, our limitations, our wounds, and even our darkness, as well as our wholeness. This time in my life, I know, allows me to enter the dark times of others with compassion.

Memphis, Tennessee, was the city of change for me in many ways. Pete and I moved there from Rome, New York, in 1976 when he got a new job in a large organization. We bought a house, I easily found work, choosing home health, which allowed me the flexibility to be available for our daughters' school events. We had some discussion about which church to join and ended up becoming part of a Lutheran church that offered a church school in which we enrolled the girls. I began a master's degree program at Memphis State, which Pete's folks generously paid for. Our lives were busy and seemingly moving forward as the marriage slowly and irrevocably fell apart. Seeing what was happening, I went into counseling and asked Pete if he would go with me. He refused, saying he didn't believe in that psychological jargon. I tried a different approach beyond sharing what I learned in counseling. I got out my Cray-Pas and large drawing pad and began. I divided the page into halves. On the left, I drew a huge vase full of brightly colored flowers in full bloom. On the right stood a person in a room with no window, behind a closed door. The doorknob was on his side of the door. Colors were grays and browns and blues. When I was done, I took the picture to him and laid it on a table.

"Pete," I said, "I want to show you this. I'm on the left. I am full of color and joy and fun and love. All there for you. On the right is a room with the door closed, the doorknob on your side. That's where I feel we are."

There was a long silence. I don't remember now if he responded right then or a bit later in conversation, but I do remember his words. "I have never trusted anyone. It leaves one too vulnerable."

I was astounded. We had been married for eleven years, had two children, had weathered numbers of storms, and he said he did not trust me with who he was. It was then I saw my path clearly.

I eventually met someone else. In December 1981, Earle and I—joined by my daughters and his son and daughter—were married in a small, quiet ceremony followed by a wonderful meal in a well-known Memphis restaurant. It was the beginning of a new chapter. Earle, my second husband, was a force. Living with him challenged me, and I grew into the fullness of myself because of him. I could do no less. Both of us lived our paths and did not shirk the journey. We were a balance for each other in the challenges that came our way. We were partners who built a relationship on love and trust that allowed us to sustain that relationship through difficult times. He told me once that he felt he could "bump up against me" and clearly enjoyed that. The first major life event in our lives came in our first ten years.

THRESHOLDS

Emotional chaos explodes inside me with the words.

"The biopsy shows two different types of cancer. You will need a mastectomy, and we can discuss reconstruction."

I blow away, tossed. What can I hang on to? The words are like dry leaves whipped by a storm, edges sharp. Thoughts fly without direction, new, fast, unexpected. Yesterday, I was a healthy, forty-nine-year-old woman, almost fifty. A seasoned health-care professional, a mother, a wife, a daughter, always healthy. In this moment, I am a diagnosis, hanging on to the mast of a tossing ship.

"Would you like me to call in Eileen? She's one of our residents and has had the same experience," Dr. Kennedy said.

"Yes," I say. Body tight. I feel myself hunching over, finding my arms to hang on to.

Eileen enters quietly. I look up and see that she is younger than I am, brown hair with no gray, slender, no white lab coat. She does not say anything, just sits down next to me and gently lays her hand on my arm. Her touch is warm and calm and steady and so kind. I feel the kindness enter me. It allows the hot tears to flow at last which melt the icy fear. She waits quietly until I'm finished. Then she talks. I don't remember the words, but they were spoken softly and brought comfort and reassurance. Beyond the words was someone taking the time to be present with me in that moment, allowing hope.

I could not name these qualities then. The quality of being present, often without words. The quality of touch, offered from kindness and caring, the quality of love conveyed through that touch. I did know, however, that I wanted and needed more.

Dr. Vasconez, my plastic surgeon, takes a long time with me and answers all my questions. There is nothing hurried about him. His voice is calm, his gaze steady, his face friendly and open. He is not much taller than I am, of medium build. His hair is black with a suggestion of gray beginning at his temples.

"Dr. Kennedy will perform the mastectomy," he tells me. "Then they will call me, and I will finish the operation by sectioning out your rectus abdominis muscle and sliding it up into the space left on your chest."

My mind goes wild with images of red bloody muscle, white tendons, my gut laid open, and I feel my muscles tighten; however, his words are so matter of fact and his voice so calm it is as though he is explaining how to boil an egg. One of the nurses later tells me he does many surgeries on children born with misshapen skulls and other bony defects. "He is known for his work with those kids," she said. I begin to see him as an artist, a sculptor, fashioning bone and flesh to create a new image.

Both doctors together did offer me options. The mastectomy is not optional because one of the cancers discovered in the biopsy is quite aggressive and does not respond well to treatment. But there are three surgical options. One is to do only the mastectomy in which case I will need to wear a prosthesis in my bra for visual balance. Second is to place a plastic prosthesis directly under the skin after the mastectomy. The third option is to do reconstruction. That is the option I choose. It uses my own flesh and will not require any prosthetics. I am a very practical person. What matters most to me is my husband's reaction to my changing body.

"What do you think?" I ask him.

"Sweetheart, I love you no matter what your choice is. My loving you does not depend on a few scars or a change in shape. I am with you all the way."

That is all I needed to hear. I have no sense of loss about the mastectomy. I am done having children. The breast is now a useless gland, so good riddance. I want to live.

Later that day, I tell my fellow faculty members. They are very supportive. I get very involved with work, aware this lets me push away the scary reality for a while.

I tell coworkers, students, and friends what is going on. It feels good to be open, not hidden, to let others in. I feel the caring of my parents, my children, and all those who surround me with their words of concern, their hugs, and offers of help. Accepting from others is an uncomfortable feeling, as though the earth I walk on is suddenly shaky, crackly, unsafe. Somewhere back in time, I learned I was supposed to be the one who took care of others. It is new to me, the sense of peace that sharing allows.

Today the usual five-mile run after work, through our neighborhood, with my husband is welcome. The rhythm of our feet rising and falling on the path is a pulse that beats a familiar melody. We talk. It is our special time.

"I feel like I am on a roller coaster. Sometimes I'm soaring, sometimes I'm terrified," I tell him.

"You will be fine," he says. 'I believe that.' His voice, his Alabama drawl, is soothing. The early fall breeze is gentle, and the brilliant reds and golds of changing leaves seem to beckon me into their bright space. I suddenly remember Dr. Kennedy's words at my last visit with him. "Take each day and event as it comes. Stay in the present," he says.

Each day is different. But the nurse telling me I will need to have a catheter for the surgery feels like a boundary has been crossed, the proverbial line in the sand. I do not want family and friends to see a pee bag hanging on the bed rail filled with yellow liquid coming from my nether parts. I want to control this. I argue with the nurse. She just looks at me and walks away.

I am left with what I cannot say out loud. I'm afraid of scaring my youngest daughter, who is still living at home. I'm afraid of dependence and restriction. I'm afraid. But then I hear a remembered melody, faint at first, beginning to build. The faculty threw a "going-to-the-hospital party" the night before the surgery, with funny cards and an evening of libations and laughter, and somewhere in the background was the sound of Jerry Lee Lewis playing his piano with hands and feet. A former classmate from the OT program called to wish me well, with the soothing soft jazz of Wynton Marsalis in the background. Others call me from all over the country wishing me the same. I am reminded of a blessing that a pastor used to give, the pastor at the church where I saw the beam of light from the cross, something about God's arms around us, supporting us, holding us. I make a conscious choice to hold that image as I am going into the operating room. The feeling of being lifted and carried and supported by the arms of loving family, loving friends, and a loving God, cradled and cared for, is a sacred symphony for all of us.

The sounds around me are different. There is beeping, someone walking in the hall, murmured voices. I hurt so badly I can hardly breathe. I see that I am back in my room. The big, round clock on the wall says it is almost twelve hours since I looked at it on the way into surgery. The pain is so bad. I find the red call button and push it.

A nurse comes in quickly. "Can I help you?"

"I am in so much pain," I say, teeth gritted together. "I can hardly move or breathe."

"You have a morphine line into your back. Have you been pushing that button?"

"I think I remember someone saying something about that, but I was afraid I would overdose myself."

"That can't happen because the machine is set to give only what you can have," she says. "I'll call Dr. Vasconez to come see you," she says, and walks out.

He was there quickly and walked directly to my bedside. Leaning over the side rail, he ever so gently pushed my bangs away from my forehead. As his hand brushed my face, like a mother's touch, I felt the pain wash away.

"I am so sorry. I will get someone here right away to take care of this pain now." His voice, calm, soothing, brought back the symphony that not many hours ago was wrapped around me with caring and love.

I saw Dr. Vasconez frequently over the next months. Until the surgical wounds were totally healed, there was always a risk of infection. First, there was the seventeen-inch incision from hip to hip which was needed to excavate the rectus abdominis muscle that became my new breast, which was fastened into the gaping hole in my chest along with its blood supply. It took well over one hundred stitches. There was no pain and never would be because nerve supply between all the parts was severed. This made frequent follow-up even more important because I no longer had the pain receptors that might warn me that something needed attention.

Dr. V., as I came to think of him, was always kind and pleasant and he seemed to have no need to move at the speed of everyone else in his busy office. He just did what he needed to do, unaware of the rolling eyes and smiles of his attendant nurses. One day, he came into the examining room with a splash of white talc across his cheek, which must have come from the inside of one of his gloves. I had to chuckle. He seemed totally unaware. He was always personable, answered my questions with clear explanations, and asked about how I was doing at work. We talked comfortably during these visits, and one day I said, "Dr. V., you're different from other doctors. I'm trying to understand why."

He seemed to know what I was talking about and said, "In my country of Ecuador we do not have the technology available that this country has to offer, so we learn other ways to help people heal."

That spoken sentence felt like a missing piece of something in my soul just dropped into place. "We learn other ways to help people heal."

I suddenly thought back to that day in the hospital, perhaps two or three days after the surgery, when I felt well enough to ask for some help with a shower and then put on a bit of lipstick and combed my hair. He walked in as I was getting settled back in my bed, looked at me, and broke into a huge smile. "You are feeling better I see." His appreciation of my cleaned-up look was clear. His reactions were genuine and were a validation for me that I was indeed getting better. A healing moment. And then the others, the touch on my forehead when I was in so much pain, the energy of his calm, kind voice laying like a warm blanket over me, comforting me when I was anxious. All of these were deliberate messages that I was seen as a well and whole person.

Thinking back to those events, now some thirty years past, I see what happened during the chaos, fear, and upheaval of a frightening diagnosis and major surgery was that I lost my self. I mourned the loss of the dream I had for my life. It was not about the loss of my breast but about something much deeper. My song of myself was about someone strong, resilient, capable, living a healthy energetic life with no fear— John Philip Sousa, "Stars and Stripes Forever," always marching forward. I was suddenly in a new reality of clashing cymbals and the thunderous, booming, powerful rumbling of tympani as I now saw only my mortality, my vulnerability, my weakness, my dependence, my loss of control.

I needed to find a new song, a new melody for my soul, which was so disrupted by this upheaval of my body, my life.

An image comes. I'm one of those hedges that when hit by a terrible cold spell looks like it's dead. But when it's chopped way back in the spring, it begins to regrow—a leaf, a twig at a time—and by midsummer is full and lush again. I am chopped down, but my leaves begin to grow again quietly, slowly pushing through the dark.

It begins. The first faint notes of a new melody from gifts of earth and sun, tendrils stirring, reaching, climbing to break through soil. I hear their whisper. Birdsongs bring lilting forms to the melody, a mixture of species weaving their unique calls in celebration as new beginnings stir. The gentle bubbling of a creek catches the birdsongs and lets them rest a bit in the ripples before the notes spring off the small waves. Insects and animals, each in their own seasons and ways, weave their voices throughout. The source of my newborn melody of self is the universe, God, nature, the elemental energy of all things.

I wonder now if the melody was already there, dormant, playing underground, eighty years ago, awakened by a cataclysmic health event.

I could not define an exact moment when the shift began. I do remember suddenly understanding very clearly that even though I had been a competent clinician for twenty-five years, I was not a healer. I started reading everything I could find about healing, remembering Dr. Vasconez's statement about finding other ways to help people heal. I also noticed a difference in my relationships with my patients. I was working in an outpatient rehabilitation clinic, and clients were varied in their issues.

One elderly gentleman was coming to me for rehabilitation after a hand injury and one day he looked at me and said, "When I come here to see you, I feel at peace."

I found myself saying, "I feel that too." That statement was offered as if coming out of the blue, without context. A bit of grace. I was able to hear it as such.

In another outpatient clinic, specializing in hand injuries, I was able to follow three other patients each for two years each because of their excellent workman's compensation insurance. Arthur was working in a sawmill when an equipment malfunction took off his left hand. Coworkers packed the hand in ice and got him to the hospital where a plastic surgeon reattached it. In my two years with Arthur, working closely with the plastic surgeon through numerous surgeries, I entered Arthur's life, and he mine. My task was to see if there was a way through strengthening and creativity to help him develop a good helper hand. He did his exercises, took part in the problem solving, and together we developed jigs which helped him stabilize an object so that he could return to making wooden toys for his children. During the first year, he came to therapy three times a week. His wife drove him, and they began bringing their elementary-age children. We became a team, a unit. He learned how to calculate the degrees of range of motion of his fingers. His children learned why he did his exercises and how they could help, and his wife filled me in on what he was doing at home. We shared stories about our dogs, our lives, and about funny things that happened. We laughed together and sometimes cried about setbacks and loss. He got stronger, was always trying to see what he could do, and proudly came in one day saying, "Look." He had brought a soft-drink can and picked it up and brought it to his mouth to drink. He was glowing with pride. We reduced the frequency of his visits, and finally, it was clear we had together reached realistic and satisfying goals. He came in for a final visit and we talked for a while.

His wife said, "Do you know what he did? He built a shed. He used his left hand in all kinds of ways as a helper."

I was totally astonished, and they were totally proud.

Then he said, "I made something for you," and brought out something wrapped in newspaper. It was a small desk calendar, the kind that has two blocks with numbers on all four sides that sit in a holder and are to be changed daily. It was sanded, stained, polished, and just beautiful. I cried. I was incredibly touched and filled with gratitude for his thoughtfulness and for all the long, careful work he did to create this very useful and appropriate gift. I kept it on my desk for decades.

Tim, the second patient, was a twenty-six-year-old policeman who was shot in the hand when he made a traffic stop and the driver pulled out a gun. The bullet entered through the palm of his hand and exited through the back, causing major destruction of the tendons. Again, there were many surgeries and a long rehabilitation. Our conversations became about work issues.

He said, "My wife wants me to quit and look for a new job. My coworkers want me to come back. You keep me in the present time. It's the caring that matters most. I feel like you are the only person who listens."

My message to him was to take just one day at a time, to stay in the present, and see how the rehabilitation progressed. It eventually came down to competency in using his firearm. I didn't know until then that police must pass annual competencies in shooting. So, I asked him to bring his pistol to therapy, and we'd see what we could do. He brought his unloaded 9-millimeter, and we worked on grasp and strength. He came in, smiling, for a final visit, saying, "I passed the competency and am going back to work."

Regina was the last of the three long-term clients. She was a middle-aged woman who worked in a factory that made O-rings. Her accident happened when the piece of machinery malfunctioned and drilled an O-ring through her wrist, causing a partial amputation. Again, the rehabilitation was very long. Regina was often depressed.

She said one day, "It's so hard. I have always been independent and the one who took care of the house and cooked and looked after the family even with my job, and now I can't do anything. I can hardly take care of myself. My family wants me to just give up. But I don't want to do that."

"Is there something that you can do that gives you some feeling of worth?" I asked her.

She thought for a minute and then said, "I can sit in the garden and there I can talk with God." Her face relaxed and looked more peaceful when she said that. "Then let's include that in your rehabilitation program. Sit in your garden twice a day, in between your exercise."

"You give me hope," she said. "You are the only one who gives me hope."

My patients were teaching me.

A transformation was taking place. My cancer led me into a much deeper and very personal understanding of healing. The first thing I tried to find was my clients' spirit. I found it in their eyes, their voice, and in what they gave back to me.

As my healing continues, the colors and richness of my life increase in quality and intensity. I see texture in fabric, in nature, in skin, in clouds, in the petal of a flower, in the sound of a melody, and in all that happens. Colors emerge from people themselves. I become able to see a person's aura or emanation of color. I come to a place of understanding how tenuous life is, how important to enjoy and live fully in each moment of each day. I experience everything differently. I see my patients differently. I am required by our medical system to document problems, but what I also list are their strengths. It is the person's strength that I look for and build on, for and with them.

In a corner of my cancer journal, which I kept for three years, was a Japanese haiku attributed to Chosu.

Broken and broken
again, on the sea
The moon so easily mends.

Are we not like that image of the moon— tossed, broken— but as the moon has substance and reality, so as the waters still, the image mends? I imagine myself as the moon, always there, always shining. And even though tossed and broken by what life brings, the mending is there as the light and substance are there.

Two other understandings come to me during this long period of healing. The less I talk while working with a patient, the more they tell me, the more they share of themselves. And somehow linked with this is touch. Touch is always involved in some way when working with people who are distressed, in pain, or needing guidance in exercise and movement. But when space is opened for people to share, space is also opened for me to hear a different conversation, the conversation of the body. I find that I can feel a person's level of stress or pain or illness. My hands become one of the instruments I use to touch their lives, to have a conversation of caring.

Years went by in this time of learning and then I was offered an opportunity. I was recruited to develop an occupational therapy program at a university in the Rio Grande Valley of Texas. With my husband's full support, I followed through and was hired. It was not long before we drove from Kentucky to Edinburg, Texas, and to a whole new way of being, living, and learning.

My thirteen years of living there became a womb of time. New things grew and changed. A new job, a new experience of life, the time between my breast cancer surgery and my husband's long time of illness and then his death. It also held the time of my immersion in Healing Touch, my growth as a healer, and my appreciation of a different culture and a new environment. Each was birthed in its own time.

I was teaching then in a university and found treasures in that part of the world that were different from other places that I had lived, such as the sound of palm branches brushing against each other in the wind off the gulf, so different from the gentler song of wind through pines in the north. There was a walk I often took in our neighborhood past the dancing mesquite trees as I thought of them. They were my favorites. They were not very tall, and their trunks grew in curves and twists that only they could imagine as they adapted to the growth around them. The wood is beautiful, dense, and red-hued. It is a wonderful wood for fires of all kinds but especially for grilling chicken and ribs. I learned about this when Elma, my neighbor, would frequently cross the street with the gift of freshly cooked meat, rice, and beans fresh from her backyard grill.

"A plate for you," she always said with a warm smile. It was given in love.

I always looked forward to passing these two special trees. Their lacey, green, pinnate leaves sheltered long, purplish pods of mesquite beans that could be ground for flour or used in everyday cooking. The trees grew side by side like siblings or friends or lovers, wrapping around each other. Their trunks seemed to move in a dance that changed and shifted as I walked by. Experiencing them was a meditation.

In my first two years in Texas, my husband and I lived apart because of job demands, visiting when we could. I lived in a duplex, which had a large backyard, in McAllen, Texas. In that yard was a huge tree with long, trailing, willow-like branches that seemed always to be moving gently in the breeze. It sheltered my two dogs, providing shade as I mowed the grass, and was a playful challenge for me as I passed beneath with branches trying to catch my hat, tugging at it. We had a relationship, the tree and me.

One evening, after dark, I felt that tree calling me. I can't describe it any other way. I certainly didn't hear voices or words but felt compelled to go outside to the yard. I walked over to the tree and wrapped my arms around the massive trunk. It was so big my arms would not reach all the way, but I suddenly felt very connected as with a living being. I stood there for a long time, my cheek against the rough bark, and felt a comfort I did not expect. I remember it as a most amazing experience. A friendship perhaps. A kinship. An introduction to what was to become a love of trees.

One of my responsibilities as program director was to order four cadavers from Texas Tech University at the beginning of every fall term, so that our students could dissect a human body, learning in a most intimate way how we work. Every year, when I walked into the cadaver lab, I felt as though I was entering sacred space. What miracles we are. What a miracle the human body is. I did not think anyone could deny the presence of God in that setting. These four individuals or their families had donated their bodies for this purpose, to be teachers for young people. My understanding of sacred space came to me in many ways.

Sight, sound, smell, taste, touch. Somewhere along the way that's what we learn as the basis of our human sensory system. In what now seems like a microcosm of time, I was swept into a world that took me way beyond those five words, and still, now, keeps teaching me, leading me into realms of knowing beyond what I could have ever imagined.

Touch has always been my touchstone. Touch. Stone. Touch, my place of connection. Stone my anchor. I have piles of stones within and around my house. Many came from Scarborough Beach in Maine, a place where I feel touched by Spirit. There I am bathed with space, light, the sound of waves, and the dancing colors that shimmer over the water. My other stones are from the Southwest. Red chunks of iron-rich rock from Sedona, Arizona, and from New Mexico, rocks and stones showing layers of sandstone, shale, and limestone, as well as basalt. Fragments from places of ancient volcanic disturbance. I feel the energy vibrating as I hold them, anchors to the earth.

I have been told that Native Americans consider rocks to be grandfathers and grandmothers and that they need to be consulted on the way of things. It is only in the relatively recent past that I am drawn to them. The incredible, magical red rocks hold the history of that land and have been shaped by wind and storm and water just as we are shaped by the storms and eddies of life. Magnificence results, in the rocks and in those who are called to them.

My youngest daughter takes me to a beach in Maine. We stand by the shore, and she says, "Listen." As the waves slide gently in, small rocks roll and tumble over each other, creating a music that I have never heard before. This natural tumbler creates smooth, round stones of all colors and striations, a blessed place. My daughter and I build cairns that day, marking our coming. There are cairns along Red Rock Creek in Sedona as well, behind Cathedral Rock. Hundreds of them are built by passersby in a natural curve of the riverbank, the stones brought by spring floods. Markers of people called to leave a trace of themselves and mark passage for others. Perhaps in my own way, I have consulted these grandmother and grandfather stones in my passing.

Within my training in occupational therapy, I begin to understand other sensory systems. Our joints hold receptors that tell us where we are in space. Pain receptors are located throughout our body. They tell us when potentially damaging stimuli appear by sending "possible threat" signals to the spinal cord and the brain. The brain creates the sensation of pain to direct attention to the body part, so the threat can be eased. Tension and stretch receptors are found in muscle and skin and warn the body of forces that may be harmful. Our balance and sense of ourselves in space are monitored by our vestibular system in order to coordinate movement. It sends signals primarily to structures that control eye movement which is closely linked to balance. Signals are also sent to the muscles that keep us upright. I learn that the pressure in my hands can create change in movement. All people have muscle tone. It is a state in which contractions continue without direction, sort of a steady state. Tone is different from person to person. At a moment in time when both of my daughters weighed the same, my older daughter, who is Asian, small boned and high toned always felt very light when I picked her up. My younger daughter who is taller, long boned, and lower in tone, always felt heavier to pick up, at the same weight. Both are normal. But people who have high tone caused by neurological disease or injury which interferes with function can experience reduction in tone when deep pressure is applied steadily to large muscle groups. My husband would often come home from work with tight muscles, especially in his shoulders and neck. I had him lie on the floor on his back and pressed my hands firmly and deeply into his pectoral muscles until I felt the muscles relax. That same technique works with children who are spastic. Their tone can be relaxed with deep pressure on specific muscles.

None of these techniques are sacred. I learned them along with my classmates. However, it seems as though my hands learned them independently of my mind. Over time, I could just touch someone and know if they were well, ill, anxious, relaxed, depressed, distracted, troubled, or happy. It just happened that way. It is still that way.

The hand is a sensory organ more powerful than our eyes and ears. They hold millions of receptors waiting to carry outside worlds inside, bringing what is inside us to the outside world. We touch the sharp, soft, fluffy, slick, resistant, yielding. Taking in with our hands we incorporate, process, then return. We give out through our hands that which might be soft, tender, harsh, dull, abrasive, hard, soothing.

As far back as I can remember, I have noticed hands. Before I had many words. Perhaps all people do that. My father comes first into my mind as I find my childhood memories. His hands were beautiful, I thought. Balanced, well-shaped, strong, coordinated in movement. They were a man's hands, but when he took my small hand to cross a busy street, they were enfolding and protective, warm, and reassuring.

They were also an artist's hands. I watched him all through my growing up as he sketched his baseball heroes on scraps of paper or sketched out plans for a piece of furniture he had in mind and then built. He was a creator. I also remember how those hands balled into fists when he had an episode of rage. That frightened me as a child but no longer dwells in my memory. Only the reassurance remains, alive and tactile still.

The first thing about my mother's hands that fascinated me as a child was her misshapen, right-index fingertip. I thought it looked so funny. She told my sister and me when we were older that once she had gotten that finger caught in a closing car door, and it nipped off a bit of her fingertip. It was not enough of an injury to interfere with function though. The next thing I remember about her hands was that the skin had a shiny look to it. Smooth and shiny. And the last big thing I remember was that for a long period of time, when I was in my early teens, she had chronic oozing fingers that she said was related to an allergy to dish detergent. It seemed to last for months and months. She had to wear white, cotton gloves and put salve on her fingers and not get them wet, so Daddy had to help her with her bath. I always thought that was how Mom showed her unhappiness.

Her hands were very capable. She was an expert typist. She embroidered a tablecloth that now is on my dining room table. It has a neat and perfectly sewn cross-stitched border. I treasure it. She kept house, she worked hard. But in all my life, I do not remember the same feeling I had when she touched me as I did when my father held my hand long ago.

My husband, first a bench research scientist, then a university administrator and faculty member, had hands that were strong and somewhat beefy, kind, and soothing. They did not really fit the world he worked in, but they fit the activities he enjoyed: fishing, paddling a canoe over rapids, racquetball, and hanging on to motorcycle bars as he found new trails.

My grandmother, my Nanny, had hands that had seen much hard work. They were broad, made for tossing strudel and tending a garden. I was fascinated by her enlarged arthritic joints and the Heberden's nodes that appeared on her finger joints, signaling the appearance of more arthritis. She never showed any signs of slowing down. They were kind hands, shaped by giving.

I look down now at my eighty-year-old hands. Well-shaped I think, well-balanced, not large, perhaps medium size, but now wrinkly. I see no signs of the arthritis that chose my knees instead. My hands have held a newborn to my breast to nurse. My hands have held my mother's and my husband's hands at the moment they left. My hands have held the hands of thousands of people with whom I have worked in my lifetime, always carrying my love and compassion.

I look for the scar I thought I would have forever in the web space between my left thumb and index finger, a fine white line. A result of my sister and I having a fight over doing dishes when we were in elementary school. It was not intended. The knife just slipped in the soapy water. *How interesting*, I think. I wonder if that is how it is with the scars of life. If enough time goes by, do they fade, disappear?

There is a small ceramic piece, seen in Mayan Indian culture, called A Circle of Friends. Generally, a small group of people stand in a circle. Their arms are around each other's shoulders, hands, fingers outstretched. All have hands that carry the story of their life, all different, yet they live in shared friendship.

With our hands, we both receive from and give to the world

around us. It is the work of our hands that weaves within the fabric of our being the tapestry of who we are. By the work of our hands, we shape the expression of our identity. Hand is creation driven by soul. It moves in a dance with the rhythms of tasks, moods, surfaces, nervous system, and energies of all that it touches. It is our connection with life.

I see now that Dr. Vasconez's statement, "We learn other ways to help people heal," came to me at a time of readiness. A time when I could hear the message. I thought about this gentle man and his gentle touch on my forehead after my surgery, a touch that felt like a mother's touch. It allowed me to focus on something other than my pain. It gave me a way through the pain to a connection with a caring person and to my own deeper self. I read everything I could find about healing and found a wide range of approaches across cultures and traditions. I also began noticing my own interactions with my patients. As I write this, I still feel how my touch became a way to hear someone without words. I could hear with my hands. I could talk to patients with my touch by altering pressure and pace of movement. I also found that I needed to make eye contact, and as time went on, this became a way to touch someone's spirit. I did that often without words but with presence.

Another signpost on my journey was my friend Sally waving a blue brochure at me, saying, "You have to go to this!" It was an announcement for Healing Touch Level I to be offered in San Antonio, only a four-hour drive north of McAllen, Texas, where I lived. My introduction to and training in Healing Touch began to gather the threads of what I had already learned and combined them with other levels of learning to create a thick, multi-colored braid of knowing that wrapped around my being, inside and out, and then lovingly connected with and wrapped around those with whom I worked.

Healing Touch is a structured program growing out of a nursing curriculum consisting of five levels of training that develop practitioner skills in management of energy flow in a body. It is a noninvasive approach in which light touch may be used, but work can be done in a person's energy field as well. The goal of treatment is the balancing of energies to encourage a deeply calm state which facilitates the client's own healing power. The client and the practitioner become energetically connected in the process, and research has demonstrated that an entrainment of heart rhythms occurs during treatment.

This is the explanation of the program, but my experiential learning felt unrelated to these words. Classes were small, perhaps a dozen of us working together for fifteen hours over a weekend for each of the first three levels. The final two levels lasted a week each. We worked in pairs with two instructors circulating among us. They demonstrated, and we practiced. The first thing we learned was to feel energy, first on ourselves and then on each other. We felt this primarily with our hands. Then we learned how to center ourselves. I remember this feeling that was so natural and familiar, so much already a part of me. The centering began with us imagining our feet reaching down into the center of the earth, and there I suddenly was with my rocks, my anchors, connected. Then we were to imagine light coming into the tops of our heads and traveling down our spines, then up into our arms and out into our hands. And there I was on the beach in Maine. Already there. The centering process quickly became part of me and still is twenty-five years later. I can just move to that place in an instant and be there. In later years, in my healing room, I often used music as a passage into that place as well.

We learned specific techniques of hand placement to move energy and we learned more about the nature of this energy. In one of the early workshops, we were in the home of one of the instructors. Furniture had been moved out of a large dining/living room area, leaving space for a half dozen massage tables. It was my turn to be on a table as other students practiced techniques on me. After we started, I heard someone say,

"Look at the fan." There was a large ceiling fan directly over me, and I looked up along with the other students. The fan was rotating steadily in a clockwise motion, almost swinging, strong enough to noticeably move the air. The switch had not been turned on, and the windows were closed. There was nothing that could have created that movement except the energy generated by what was happening between me and those working on me. A learning. Shortly after that, one of the instructors, who would later become my mentor, said, "Oh, I see an angel just outside the door." We all continued working. Suddenly, I felt small hands, perhaps the size of a five-year-old's, patting me gently all over my back with quick, light pats. I remember it feeling rather delightful. Then I felt a warm presence lie down on the table next to me, the length of my body. It felt warm and golden. The sensation lasted perhaps a minute or two and then was gone. We talked about experiences like this at the end of each workshop. There was no attempt to explain these things, no need to. They were part of the mystery of entering a spiritual place with your client and trusting that whatever came forth was meant to. What I learned quickly was that all I had to do was to center myself, be fully present with that person, and then get out of the way to allow the energy to work. As I became more practiced, there were many times when I knew there were other beings in the room with me, including Christ, Archangel Michael, and sometimes legions of others whom I did not know except that they were there in service and support of the client. This work always felt holy to me.

There are three lessons within my time with Healing Touch that stay with me and have guided me through all the time in between. An occupational therapy colleague, who was also a Healing Touch practitioner, and I had been accepted as presenters at our annual state occupational therapy conference in

San Antonio, Texas. Our topic was Healing Touch. My co-presenter, Pat, was already a certified instructor and was going to start the session with information about background, concept, and definition, and I was to follow with experiential examples. I sat quietly in the front of the room as people filed in, waiting for my turn to present. I was feeling quite relaxed, just observing people. I noticed two women come in who seemed to be friends. They sat about halfway back. One of the women looked physically very uncomfortable. She often looked down, occasionally rubbing her eyes and forehead. She periodically talked to her friend who looked concerned. A migraine, I thought. A knowing. My mother had them periodically, and I had one once. It was not comfortable. I remember feeling for that woman, appreciating how much pain she must have been experiencing. My heart went out to her. I then tuned back to what Pat had been talking about and the program went on. After the session ended, the woman who had seemed in distress came up to me and said, "I want to thank you. I had a terrible migraine, and you looked at me, and when you did, it just went away. It's gone." She looked relaxed, was smiling, and then said how grateful she was. I didn't know what to say except "thank you." This was my learning about the power of compassion which, as I grew in my skill, became an integral part of healing. Compassion can be a formal statement of intent but also a response of the heart. Both are necessary parts of the patient/therapist relationship. I think the learning example for me was that I had no cognitive thought about doing anything, but my heart had its own knowing.

I am suddenly taken to the story of Jesus healing a woman who came up behind him and touched his robe. This miracle is recorded in Mark 5:25-34, Luke 8:43-48, and Matthew 9:20-22. Jesus did not see the occurrence but was aware of a change in energy. As it was told, he asked who had touched him, and the woman spoke identifying herself. Again, it was told that he spoke directly to her giving her his full attention and acknowledging that her faith had healed her. I am immediately back in the church pew at fifteen sitting in the presence of Jesus, who was fully present to me.

The second lesson involved my husband, who had three motorcycle incidents before I drew my line in the sand. He had been out riding and was waiting to pull out onto a highway when his front wheel slid on some gravel, and down he went. One of his feet got caught, causing a crush injury to his forefoot. He was frightened and in a lot of pain. We went to the ER, and he was sent home with directions to elevate and ice. I went into the bedroom to rest. Sometime in the time of resting, I began to feel a very strong pull to go to my husband and lay my hands on his foot. I had to go. I sat on a chair next to his elevated leg, gently wrapping both hands around his forefoot with the intention of sending energy from my hands into his foot. I stayed there for perhaps twenty minutes. As I held his foot, I could feel movement inside of it. I also felt what seemed like electricity occasionally moving between my hands as well. He said that he could feel those things too. My intention for healing was there, and I had learned to just wait until it seemed I was done. Gradually his foot felt cooler, as did my hands, and I knew I was done. He said his foot felt better, and the next day much of the swelling and bruising was gone. When all five levels of training were completed, I was required to complete a one-year mentorship with a seasoned practitioner. Mine was Mary Frost, a gifted and caring guide. I called her the next day and told her what happened with my husband and about the strange feeling of being pulled off my bed to go place my hands on my husband's foot. She simply said, "You were being taught."

The third learning happened with a woman who had been coming once a week for some time with several involved issues. She was scheduled for a Saturday morning, and I woke up that morning feeling not well at all. I called her to cancel the appointment, worried that I might have something contagious (which I did) but could not reach her. She arrived on time, and I explained that I was not feeling well and said if she felt that she needed to just go home that was fine. She said that she wanted to stay. I worked with her for the full hour but felt that I had not been able to give her an adequate session. It bothered me. Again, I called Mary. Again, her comments were short. She just said, "Judy, people take what they need." It was that simple. My learning was I was not the captain of the ship. It was not me that made things happen. It was grace.

Three learnings. The power of intention and compassion. I am always being taught. I am only a conduit for the flow of energy.

In the years I was involved in training and then practicing Healing Touch as a Certified Practitioner, additional doors opened for me and never shut. I was hungry for the learning. Each wave filled spaces I did not know were there. Medical Intuitive Training I and II taught by Kim Seer, CHTP, and Kathy Sinnett, RN, HNC, CHTP/I, were designed to deepen the practitioner's intuitive skills in identifying physical, mental, and emotional blocks in the energy field and in the body itself. Using quantum energy principles, the practitioner learns to release and remove these blocks at the source. I found this a whole new way of "seeing," allowing me to see into the body itself. What most people understand as "seeing" is physical, using the eyes, but intuitive seeing uses inner vision or an inner "knowing."

Therapeutic Communications: Energetic Interventions, taught by Sharon Scandrett-Hibdon, RN, PhD, was a guide in refining communication skills in a way that supports the client in self-discovery and positive self-regard. Learning to read energetically what might arise in a healing session and respond consciously and in a disciplined way allows us to respond to the client most helpfully.

Experiential Anatomy and Physiology for Healers, Levels I and II, was taught by Sue Hovland, RN, CHTP and Certified

Massage Therapist. It focused on deeper understanding of body tissues and systems, then applying that knowledge to energetic healing. The process of learning how to locate, energetically palpate organ and endocrine systems, and then feel how energy moves through our entire body brings a concept of the whole, the miracle of every molecule, every organ, and every system working together and is also the miracle of the soul.

I was fortunate during this period of learning to take part in two different but related workshops. The first was Cranio-Sacral Therapy I, developed by Dr. John Upledger, and the second was a ten-day series of classes with John F. Barnes, PT, in Myofascial Release. Both approaches use intuitive knowing and gentle touch to release blocks of movement in the human body. The Upledger approach focuses on the cranio-sacral system which is essentially a hydraulic system of the dura mater that envelops the brain and spinal cord. Cerebral spinal fluid is produced within this system to bathe and nourish the brain and nervous system. Normally, there is a continuous rhythmic flow of fluid pressure that holds the system in balance. But if the system is not functioning normally, the pressure can build and damage the central nervous system. The cranio-sacral approach uses touch no heavier than the weight of a nickel to intuitively identify the areas of restriction and then sense what the body needs to do to release the obstruction. It is a therapy of intuitive listening to the body and then follows with the movement the body is asking for. The Myofascial Release program also uses the same measure of light touch, directly on the skin, to identify areas of fascial restriction. Fascia is connective tissue that wraps around muscle. One can see it as a white film attached to a beef roast. It is generally able to be flexible and resist great unidirectional tension forces. But it can also tighten and resist forces, causing stress and pain. With that lightest of touches, it is possible to feel the tightness of the fascia and then gently and slowly begin to loosen and guide it into a different pattern, releasing the stricture.

"Never forget the importance of remembering the awe and wonder of life." She stood in front of an assembled audience of perhaps a thousand physicians. A small woman with very dark hair, she had a radiance about her. Her words fit my own mind-set. This was my introduction to Dr. Rachel Naomi Remen, speaking at an alternative medicine conference in Florida per-haps fifty years ago. Since then, I continue to learn from her through her books, articles, and teaching. She talks about how medicine is so focused on getting back to the way we were. We forget the gentle art of letting go, allowing us to meet the new, -to meet the future. She teaches the importance of imag-ination and imagery in dealing with illness. She herself has a chronic illness and has had many serious surgeries and devel-oped a program to teach physicians how to be healers. The theme throughout her work is that spirit is an essential need of human nature. She writes of the difference between help-ing, fixing, and serving and asks a question of all of us. Is it possible for any of our senses to become a doorway to sacred experience?

The phrase, being open to awe and mystery, was so affirm-ing for me because that ability, that openness was also some-thing that seemed to gallop out of the birth canal alongside curiosity. It feels much like the wonder of a child experienc-ing Disney World for the first time or the first time I looked down into the Grand Canyon and felt tears running down my face at the majesty of God's creation. I feel that every day in some way.

There was a time, many years later, when I was taking part in a workshop based on a book called *The Artist's Way*, by Julia Cameron. The meetings were held at a Unitarian Universalist Church in town. I was drawn to become part of this when art-ist friends of mine encouraged me to attend. My own church did not offer such programs, and I had been looking for a new perspective on my painting and writing. This, together with my own innate curiosity about new people and beliefs drew me. A part of that workshop involved daily writing, first thing in the morning, of three handwritten pages of stream-of-consciousness thought. I did that faithfully for weeks and weeks, and one day I looked down and saw a word appear that was profound for me. It was the word "allow." Suddenly, I found myself starting to print that word in larger and larger letters. And then I began to say it. ALLOW. I opened my mouth wider and spoke the word louder, feeling how it felt in my mouth to say it. Feeling how my tongue was placed, how my throat opened to accommodate the flow of air, how my diaphragm pushed the air upward and out from my center. That word has become a part of me, a part of my truth every day since. As I think back over my many decades, I think that the capacity to be open, to permit, to provide opportunity, to make space for, to make provision for, or provide scope for something was birthed with me along with curiosity and wonder. A triumvirate of joy.

I was also drawn into several years of study of traditional Chinese medicine under the auspices of the Traditional Chinese Medicine World Foundation based in New York City. The founder and developer, Master Nan Lu, was trained in the Taoist tradition in the lineage of two significant teachers and has spent his life supporting the integration of traditional Chinese medicine with conventional Western medicine in a broad, integrative health-care context. He supports the strengths of TCM in ways that complement Western medicine in a philosophy of health and prevention that encompasses body, mind, and spirit.

There was a time, in a week-long TCM workshop in upstate New York, when I saw something remarkable. We were all taking a break; the day was lovely, and most of us went outside. I happened on Master Lu leaving the building and heading into the woods. I can only describe the feeling. It was as though he became part of the woods. He was fully present, walking with purpose into welcoming branches. He was no longer part of this world. It felt like I was watching a sacred moment.

For approximately twenty-five years, I was immersed in learning about healing from a wide variety of sources that came to me. It was a period of openness to the learning and an immersion in application of new approaches and concepts. Intuition, compassion, knowing, and skill grew without my even being aware. I became part of that world. I am still part of that world. I think of Hildegard von Bingen, cemented into her cell as a child, immersed in the learning provided for her by her Bible, her herb garden, and the monk who supplied her with books from the monastery library. Out of that small physical space, she created amazing gifts of music, poetry, healing and eventually created a new path for women in her world.

I feel kinship with her still. All the teachers that appeared for me taught me what came to be a new series of Bible stories. The twenty-five years of learning was—and still is—a Bible for me in this modern day. It lives as an accompaniment to the Bible I grew up with. The foundation, the underlying melody that played through those years was the Presence of Christ in that church in Allentown when I was fifteen. The Presence that for me was sitting with the man, the person who was the Christ, who was a healer, a fountain of love and compassion, and who is present for each person on this earth.

I find threads that connect me, the child, with me, the adult. I found a photograph of my mother and myself taken when I was four at the most. My mother stands, looking like a wooden statue with no sense of movement. Her hand, holding mine, is the same configuration as the other hand holding her purse.

Her face is vacant of expression. I look at my face in the photo and I see that I am already lost from her. My blessing is having an unconditionally loving grandmother who lived on the same street. She was my anchor. Solid, uncomplicated, connected to her garden, her flowers, her cooking, and her family. I found other anchors in the natural world. Stones, animals, trees, grasses, streams, light, sound. I found my own words for my world. Inner voices. They carry me still.

Sometime after I began my training in Healing Touch—I'm not sure exactly when—I began having dreams that I was a member of a robed, religious community. The robes in my dreams were brown and long. They felt heavy and rough. The community would meet in a place that was outdoors in a wide, gently hilly space where there was singing as well as discussion. I felt like I knew the people. After a few of these dreams, I mentioned them to my friend Sally.

"Judy," she said. "I have used a psychic from time to time and she may be able to help you find some answers. I'll look up her phone number for you."

"Thank you," I said.

I called the woman, who lived in California, and we set up an appointment to last an hour. She spoke with a British accent. One of the things she told me as we moved into the session was, "I see you as a monk in the time of the Inquisition. You had special gifts such as clairvoyance and had to flee into caves in the hills to avoid imprisonment and possibly death at the hands of the Inquisition." Although we dealt with other things during the session, the image of myself as a monk, a cloistered being, felt real to me. It is the part I remember in a way that is still vivid.

Recently, I contacted another person, highly credentialed with a long history in health care. She is a medical doctor who was intuitive from birth and has been called a Mystical Physician. She believes that healing and illness are soul-centered issues. I set up an appointment. During that discussion, I told her about my long-ago session with the psychic. This was her response as an intuitive:

"You were more than just a monk though. You were a highly evolved priest. You were carrying the wisdom, mysteries of your priesthood. You were a keeper of wisdom. You were translating or transcribing or carrying the stories of the Bible to keep it alive. These monks were hidden even from their own monasteries. You carried the mythologies, the stories of your people through many lives. It's almost why you are a storyteller and that's why you are here, but you are even weaving into a much larger story."

I suddenly was carried back to my earliest memories. Being alone often as a child but not feeling lonely, comfortable with my own thoughts and imagination. Needing time and space, always. A need that was not understood by my family. The joy of having my own attic room when I was fourteen. My cell, my place of solitude, contemplation, writing, drawing. My long period of wishing for a cloistered life after my experience with Christ at fifteen. My persistent need until the writing of this book was to protect what I knew and experienced, to not share. My curiosity all my life about people, different cultures, healing, a world wider than my hometown, the street on which I lived. A wonder about the world, nature, the universe, animal life. The persistent need to periodically withdraw into quiet space, nature, a place of meditation when life became too busy.

Three times I came here. It was the year my husband was dying. The first time I entered my room in this silent retreat center in Sarita, Texas, all I saw was white. A single window covered with a white cloth curtain let in only a suggestion of late afternoon light. I came hoping for a place to allow the release of and freedom from tension that had come to fill my body. As my eyes adjusted to the dim light, I saw that the furnishings were spare: a single bed, a brown dresser, a brown recliner, a brown desk with a small lamp, and a desk chair. I saw a narrow shower stall, toilet, and sink tucked into a small alcove. The walls were bare except for a large wooden cross hung on the wall. *I want to stay here for a very long time*, I thought, as I felt the tension I had been holding for years, it seemed, leave my body in a very, very long exhale. I spent my time there on long walks on trails through Texas scrub brush, feeling connected to the animals who felt safe there and so did not run. Armadillos made their slow way through the grasses, javelinas trotted down paths they knew, an occasional Texas Longhorn appeared from behind a tree (huge animals up close), and myriads of birds and turkey vultures circled in the evening skies as they settled in to find a roosting place in the palms. Wild turkeys and deer ambled along the roads, and at night the coyotes sang. I spent time here journaling and allowing myself to be present with myself.

Memories of this place and the peace it brought me wound around and through my years of doing Healing Touch. They became resident reminders of contemplative life by teaching me how to prepare for the mysteries I found in energetic communication. The space I entered with my clients felt as peaceful and sacred for me as for them.

I had heard the word "shape-shifter" from time to time. It seemed to gather a variety of meanings that also shifted in shape over time. I wondered if I was a shape-shifter. Had I become a shape-shifter after practicing Healing Touch for so many years?

I see healers as shape-shifters, constantly shifting the shape of our experience with words, touch, music, and energy. For me, it feels like a holy moment between two people in which our shared inner and outer experiences become integrated. I think it is a common occurrence in healing work.

Thinking over the years, so many people stand out for me

as my experiences unfolded. I wonder if I was a shape-shifter through it all. Three of my clients come to mind now.

Dr. Simonson and I had known each other for a while as I sat on a board with him and was involved in some shared community activities as well. He was a psychologist in Edinburg, Texas, well respected as an advocate for mental health and healing and had referred several people to me and then finally himself. He was in his eighties then and had end-stage prostate cancer. Most of the Healing Touch work I did with him was balancing his energy flow and holding intention for relaxation and healing. One day when he arrived, I, as usual, walked with him along the path to my healing room as he pushed his walker. He looked troubled. I helped him up onto my table and asked if he had any focus for the session.

"I'm so frustrated with the pain and aching in my feet. I don't know what to do about it. I just don't know what to do."

I found myself saying, "Let's make today's session about being in gratitude for your feet and for the many, many miles they have faithfully carried you through your years. I will hold that intention as I work and I ask you to join me in that thought."

"I will," he said.

I always let my clients come out of their deep relaxation on their own time. When he opened his eyes, I helped him sit up and asked how he felt.

"I think I feel better," he said. He did not say much more as I helped him off the table and across the yard to his car. But the space between and around us felt much smoother and quieter.

I only worked once with Johnny who was referred to me by another psychologist. He was a nice-looking young man in his late twenties. I asked him what he would like to work on.

"I have had pain in my right hip for years. It has been

there since I had a skiing accident years ago, and no one has been able to find a reason or solution. It's just always there." He looked frustrated.

I talked a bit about what my idea of working with energy was and what I was going to do.

He got on the table, and I began some preliminary relaxation techniques that involved smoothing the energy field and then started a more structured energy balancing that involved light touch at specific energy points. I was centered, just allowing, and noticing what I was feeling in the energy flow. When I came to his hips, I placed a hand on each of his hips to move energy between them through my hands. Suddenly the massage table that he was on began banging against my leg. I looked down and saw the table move. It bounced off my leg hard enough to be uncomfortable. I looked at Johnny, and he looked deeply relaxed.

It was then I smiled to myself and knew I was not the one working on him. The table shaking went on for several minutes, and when it stopped, I tuned back into the structure of treatment that I had started.

When Johnny roused from his deep relaxation, he sat up, and I asked him how he felt.

"I feel good," he said.

"Did you feel the table moving at all?" I asked.

He said, "No."

"Wow," he said as he got up and started to walk to the door. "The pain is totally gone."

Was I a shape-shifter in this or was someone else?

I had been working in a traumatic hand injury clinic for several years when I met Jim, referred to me by one of the plastic surgeons as someone who was going to need a long rehabilitation process.

Jim had been a chemical engineer for a large firm in California. After much self-searching, he decided to leave that position to join a band as a guitarist, a longtime passion of his. He was successful in this group and played with them for several years. On a road trip across the country, he was involved in an auto accident that gravely damaged the extensor tendons in his left hand, the hand that wrapped around the frets of the guitar. The surgeon and I worked together for many weeks through several surgeries to repair the tendons and keep scar tissue at bay. After each surgery, I worked with Jim on regaining motion and got to know him well. He always arrived in blue jeans, boots, sometimes a vest. He wore his light brown hair long, and it sometimes looked a bit scraggly. He talked about whether he could go back to playing with his band, given his injury, and said he could not get any information from his surgeon.

Jim's wife often came to therapy with him. She was a quiet person but clearly very supportive of her husband. I began to see that to move on with their lives, adapt, and make decisions, they needed to know what the result of his injury would be.

The surgeon, Dr. Drake, came and talked to me as well.

'I just don't seem to be able to connect with Jim. He's a nice guy, but we just don't connect.' He seemed as frustrated as Jim.

The next time Jim came to therapy I asked him if he remembered what it was like when he worked as a chemical engineer and had to engage with his team to discuss a problem.

He looked a bit puzzled and then said, 'Yes.'

'Let's try something,' I said. "The next time you meet with Dr. Drake, wear a suit and tie, brush and pull your hair back, and think how it was to walk into one of those meetings at the company you worked for. Then look at the doctor and ask him exactly what you need to know from him." Jim walked out, still looking a bit puzzled, but said he would.

After his next appointment with the doctor, he came to the therapy room, looking relieved. "How did it go?" I asked.

"It went well. I was surprised. He told me I would not be able to play the guitar again, which I had suspected, but hearing him say that was a relief because now my wife and I can figure out what we need to sort out and plan for. It was very helpful."

Dr. Drake also came and talked to me. "That was the best talk I have ever had with Jim. We got down to some issues that were serious to him and we talked them all out." He looked truly pleased at how things had gone.

This is how I understand shape-shifting. Allowing a space to open or creating such a space is an opportunity for a person to find a different perspective, a connection, a relationship with another, a path toward healing.

In my years of doing Healing Touch, the way in which I felt and guided a client's energy allowed such spaces to open for them to find their own healing. Conversation after the session often supported or reinforced for them what had happened. I think many people do this during their lives, especially those involved in working with people in situations based on creating a relationship of trust. An allowing.

In my experience, patients want spiritual input. They want to know about meaning and purpose. They want to know and experience connectedness. They want an appreciation for the sacred.

Healer and healee come together in common need and common offering allowing an altered state of consciousness.

This state of deep relaxation allows space to open, inviting mental images to appear.

Imagery, which may not be present to the senses in the moment or perhaps has never been perceived before is allowed. It is a creative space, so apparent in children but sometimes seems lost as we grow into adulthood.

The use of imagery, imagination as a way of thinking, I believe, is always with us and can be triggered by simple questions or prompts, such as, "Can you imagine?" "Is there another way to look at this?" "Does this bring a memory?"

I recently ran a workshop on creating icons. This was held in conjunction with a large ICONS exhibit in the church I attend. There were over 175 pieces on display, and the last day of the exhibit featured a parish retreat. The icons workshop was part of this event. There were about a dozen participants, mostly adults, from a variety of backgrounds. The common factor was the exposure everyone had to the art pieces in the exhibit and the understanding of this art form's place in the divine mystery of worship. The goal of the workshop was for every participant to create their own personal travel icon, a small work, about 8 inches by 8 inches that could be tucked into a purse or bag that would always be there as a focus for meditation or prayer. An assistant priest and I coordinated the supplies, our roles, and the space needs. I would run the workshop.

The participants would have only one hour, and materials were very simple. Each person was given an 8-inch-by-8-inch wooden plaque. Acrylic paints, brushes, scissors, and glue guns were readily available, as were leaves and twigs we had harvested in the fall weather. Small medallions of various saints were also available should people wish to use them.

I had made two sample works which I brought to give people some idea of the variety of directions one might go. The night before I also filled a small plastic tub with all kinds of odds and ends from my home: bits of wire, yarn, thread, tissue paper of all colors, Q-tips, small reflective glass beads and buttons, and scraps of material of a variety of patterns and colors among other things.

When we came together to begin, I spent perhaps five minutes orienting everyone to where supplies were, telling everyone they were free to use anything at all. The room was a bit noisy as people moved around, getting their bearings.

Then I made these comments.

"There is no right or wrong."

"Your work is an expression of your own unique idea of the icon you are creating."

"Every person here is a creator."

"Look at the icon as though you are seeing the divine in yourself."

After that, the room became very quiet, and the participants focused quickly. I spoke only when asked a specific question. I answered briefly and to the few who seemed unsure, I responded that they needed to let go of their thoughts and let the icon speak to them. "Listen to the icon," I said.

Rodney, the church organist, a gifted musician, teacher, and singer seemed quite stuck as to where to begin. We had known each other for a decade. I don't know where my words or thoughts came from, but I looked at him, walked over to the bin of materials I had brought and pulled out my personal paintbrush. I brought it to him.

"Rodney," I said, "This is my personal paintbrush. I painted the two sample pieces using only this brush. It is magic. If you use it, you will create anything you wish." He took it without a word, walked off to another smaller room, and by the end of the hour had created a beautiful, distinctive, three-dimensional icon.

A participant whom I sat next to for a while, looked at me, smiled, and said, "I never thought of using material this way. This pattern reminds me of where I love to walk in the woods, and it just seemed right." Another participant, whom I had known for many years, became transformed. I happened to look at her as she worked, and she looked more peaceful and relaxed than I had ever seen her. She was totally absorbed. Her face, which usually looked tense, guarded, or worried, was smooth and glowing. I told her this some weeks later when we met over coffee.

"I was in my center," she said.

Everyone who participated voiced excitement and pleasure at what they had created, and some told me later how pleased their families were as well.

Everyone imagines. It's one of the major ways we think. A healer is a guide within the process, supporting the learning and growing and changing.

Looking back over this workshop, these elements of shape-shifting, as I understood them, emerged.

The environment was new. It was an upstairs room, oddly shaped, long, and narrow that was usually used for children's Sunday school.

Some participants knew me; some did not.

The materials provided were not standard "art room" materials.

Only one goal was stated. "Create a small piece of work that is spiritually personal to you."

I held the space. This is an expression that is becoming used more frequently, especially within the work of healers in a variety of professions.

I sat or moved quietly around the room. I turned off my words. I listened with an open heart. I was fully present, paying attention without intervention. I observed their process and saw most of the work but made no judgment. I got out of the way, so each person could make their own choices, respecting that they were their own guides. I gave them space to find their own voice.

These elements are involved in the shape-shifting and healing process within Healing Touch. I am sure in many other professions as well. It is the creating of space which allows people to find their own voice, their own healing in a setting that carries no expectations. The "allowing" that allows a person to let go in however long their time of pain lasts or how long it might take them to untie their knots. I think back to Jim in the hand clinic in Kentucky who just needed a suggestion as to how to think of himself in a different way to be able to open his heart of fears that ultimately allowed his doctor to give him the answers he needed. It was a reimagining of himself.

I understood and experienced all these elements at fifteen, which have become the bedrock of my being. What I didn't have at that age was the maturity to see and understand their impact on my life.

Every person has the power to heal. What gets in the way in the world we live in now is our incessant need to tell people how they should be. We are a nation of "tellers." We want to fix people. We want to give suggestions as to how to be better. We are judgmental. We don't remember compassion and we don't remember to have self-compassion. We forget that it is OK to cry and grieve with others as they struggle through their messy lives. We forget that we just need to offer our hand. In my experience of Christ, He was always present, always compassionate, without judgment.

I went through a period of years reading much of the Buddhist teacher Pema Chödrön's work. She tells us the truth is that things don't really get solved. They come together and fall apart. Then they come together again and fall apart again. It's just like that. The healing comes from letting there be room for all of this to happen, room for grief, for relief, for misery, for joy.

There are simpler ways many of us use to find a bit of space to allow new imaginings. As a child, I enjoyed watching my father create and build furniture. It was joyful for him but there were times when he got stuck as he rarely used plans. When this happened, he'd just get up from his workbench, go upstairs, get a cold Yuengling beer out of the fridge, take it out to the back porch where he'd sit in the wooden chair he built and painted apple green and sip. By the time the bottle was empty, he had worked out the problem, went back down to his basement workshop, and continued with his new solution.

For myself, I must have learned as soon as I could walk to just walk off somewhere else, maybe to another room, outdoors, or a walk along the Jordan River that ran in front of our house. As I grew older, it was always nature in both its complexity and its simplicity that allowed me to find a different view of my troubles.

Other people might use music, dance, reading a new book, painting, cooking or cleaning a closet. The ways available to guide people into new ways of seeing and ultimately healing are as varied as everything in the world around us, much of which we have probably packed away in the dark compartments of our minds.

I come back to the words "imagery" and "imagination" when I think about my long fascination with Sedona, other parts of Arizona, and later, New Mexico: Looking back from my eight-decade perspective, I suddenly see connections that also link me with healing and creativity.

The connections begin in Allentown, Pennsylvania, where I was born and grew up. It is one of the many cities that took shape in the Susquehanna River Valley. The river, which originates in central New York, drains the Appalachian Plateau of Pennsylvania and ends in Maryland where it empties into Chesapeake Bay. Settlements and communities developed in the early and mid-1700s. Industries grew from the environment. Timber, lumber, mining of coal, agriculture, textiles, and paper were a few. The mountainous areas became tourist attractions, including 2,194 miles of the Appalachian Trail. Trees are abundant. Birch, dogwood, maple, hemlock, elm, oak, sumac, and white pine heavily blanket the mountains as well as lower elevations. A painting instructor once referred to Pennsylvania skies as a particular vista.

"What do you mean?" I asked.

"The air is so saturated with moisture that the skies are rarely crystal clear," she replied. This same abundance of moisture brings winter cold so damp it breathes through the heaviest coats. Humid summers encourage rivers melting down the sides of ice cream cones.

My grandparents were part of the influx of immigrants to Allentown in the late 1800s providing an abundance of people hungry for any kind of work. They supported growth of new industries: silk mills, jute mills, Mack trucks, Bethlehem Steel, electronics, technologies, and the farmer's markets of the Pennsylvania Dutch communities. My grandfathers, father, and uncles, rose before the sun to trudge off, grizzled, in dark work clothes, carrying their aluminum lunch pails as they walked or rode buses to their jobs in wire mills, Mack truck plants, Bethlehem Steel, and tool-and-dye industries. My grandmother was a trimmer in a silk mill. Almost everyone left school to help large families bring home wages.

I knew clearly by the age of ten that I would leave as soon as I could. I knew that the place where I lived was not enough. I did not have the words then, but my heart knew.

My first visit to Sedona was like the moment the participants in the icons workshop walked through the door into the space which was sometimes a Sunday-school room for children, but was their entry into imagination and creativity, personal to each.

There is one word that comes to me when I think about the Southwest. It is "space." Huge, vast, open space. It invites me. Calls to me to explore. It invites and allows discovery of rich color, a symphony of sound and the smell of earth, trees, and plant life. We share that space with birds, animals of all kinds, fungi, creeping creatures, and many forms of life still unknown. It was that need for space that already spoke to me by the age of ten and probably earlier as I walked along the creek next to my house, as I picked up the magazine *Arizona Highways*, as I got lost in Zane Grey's description of life in the Southwest. I was born with the need for that connection with sacred space, for connection with the universe. It was when I found it on my first trip to Arizona for a conference in my thirties that the persistent beckoning began. I could not stay away from the space, the clear, dry air; the rich colors of the earth, rock, and sky in all their conversations.

I used to think there was something wrong with me. I loved painting. I still do. It used to worry me that all I seemed to paint were landscapes, skies, rolling fields of grain, seascapes, mesas, varieties of cactus, and more skies. People noticed and said, "You don't paint many people." I didn't. I don't worry anymore. I simply paint what I am led to paint. That which nourishes me. Everything that touches my heart. In Sedona, I painted space, clouds, mesas, colors, light, rock, prickly pear cactus, birds, and my Shawnee friend, David.

My husband and I traveled together to Sedona after we bought into a timeshare. We both loved it there for many of the same reasons. The last visit we made together was in 2005, two years before his death. Although his health in those years did not allow him to hike and the altitude, at 4200 feet, restricted even long walks in town, we enjoyed the beauty of the place, the good food, and the experience of being away from the East Coast. My memories of that time with him are sweet and touching. For me, it was a time of learning how to begin to let go of someone who was very ill.

We stayed at our timeshare in town which was lovely. There were paths and sidewalks that were easily navigable with views of the magnificent red cliffs everywhere one looked. Attractive plantings of native species of cactus, trees, and even lush bushes of rosemary were everywhere. And overall was the amazing big open sky, holding all the blue of the heavens above.

Every Tuesday evening, a Native American named Vernon Foster, whose tribe was Klamath Modoc, came to the time-share with his wife, Marion, who was Lakota Sioux. Their two teenage daughters came along to demonstrate dances I had never seen before. As people walked into the large, open lobby, Vernon played his light-brown wooden flute, fingers moving easily, covering the holes until it appeared that everyone who was coming was there and seated. The music was soothing, lilting, inviting, notes flowing as easily as breath.

I had come to love Native flute music. David Wolf's Robe, another person I met on my visits to Sedona, also came to the timeshare to present an evening of flute music once a week. We became friends over time. He was Shawnee and shared his knowledge easily with everyone.

"I make my own flutes," David said to me one day after his performance was over. "Would you like to see the workshop where I make them?"

"Yes, I would," I said, curious.

We made an appointment to meet a few days later at his workshop a few miles from the timeshare. The space was small, once a garage, and was organized and neat. David had a lathe and other specialized tools, but he clearly prided himself on his skill at handcrafting the flutes.

"I use a variety of woods, red cedar and black walnut, among others. Each one has its own tone, and I find it in the wood as I work." He continued with energy, reflected in the pride with which he spoke. "They can be keyed in a range of two octaves, and you can see they all have six finger holes. When I press my finger over the openings, I block off the flow of air, allowing notes to be formed within the inner space."

"This is all amazing to me," I said. "I had no idea of the complexity."

He said, "Oh yes, every handmade flute is different, and it takes a great deal of time to learn the sound and vibration of each instrument. Flutes can be made in a variety of sizes and lengths too, and each one has its own voice." He spoke eagerly, almost reverently about what he did. As I listened to the cadence, tone, and energy of his voice as he talked about his flutes, I began to hear the music of his voice. It began to flow, entering the space of that small garage. The flutes were his creations. I understood that. It was the way I felt about my paintings.

I began to develop an ear for the sounds. I could hear the light and lilting courting song. And then I was surprised at the deep, low moans of a bear or the high sound of an eagle. I felt connection with Hildegard von Bingen's music when I heard murmurs of nature, echoes of caves, the trill of birds.

Vernon's flute, both melodic and meditative, drew me back into the room. He and his wife were dressed casually, he in blue jeans, work shirt, and vest, with his black hair held back by a folded, brown bandana wrapped around his crown. His wife wore a long skirt with matching top, the colors like the earth.

Vernon began talking about his world. "We value and respect all living things. We live in gratitude for the gifts of nature and the strength of community and we live and share equally with all life forms." He and his wife sang and drummed which somehow seemed to echo the values they talked about. I could clearly hear the heartbeat of the rhythm of the drums. Boom, dub, dub, boom dub, dub, boom dub, dub.

Stepping forward, Vernon then introduced his daughters.

"A popular dance for women is the butterfly dance which my daughters will now dance for you." They were dressed in long, bright skirts and brightly decorated tops, and each wore a long shawl with even longer tassels which they held across their shoulders, arms outstretched as they danced to the beat of the drums and the songs of their parents. They spun in circles with tassels flowing and waving like butterfly wings. Their footwork was intricate with fast high steps, black braids flying. It felt like pure joy.

Vernon and his wife had brought a small child, maybe two and a half years old. I learned later that they were taking care of him temporarily while his young parents worked out some issues between them. He stood next to Vernon's wife, who put a drumstick in his little hand, and while she was drumming, she invited him to join in, which he did with gusto. Ahh, I thought. What a gentle and natural way to teach.

Vernon also talked about healing practices of Native Americans which I found very interesting. I went up to him after the presentation and talked to him about Healing Touch as I saw similarities. He listened, looked at me for a moment, and then said, "You are an Indian in white skin. I am going to have a sweat lodge at my house tomorrow night. You are welcome to come."

I said, "I would like to." It happened that easily.

The drive to Vernon's house in Cornville, just outside of Sedona, was short. His wife had given me directions the evening before. It was still light, and I found the one-story, beige-brick home in a small development. The yard was dusty with a scatter of cactus, creosote bush, and sage. I noticed ants were very busy as I walked along the path to the front door. One of his daughters answered my knock and invited me into a spacious living room ringed by long black leather couches. My eye was caught by a light tan deer hide covering one wall. Figures and animals were painted on it.

"What is that?" I asked.

"That's the story of my father's life," she said simply.

I found myself wanting to know more about that, but there was no time. Drums, a pair of Longhorn horns, and paintings with a western theme decorated other walls. I sat on one of the couches.

I was surprised that others were already gathered, a small Japanese tour group and a couple of other white people. We waited quietly for Vernon, who finally arrived from another commitment, dressed in jeans, cowboy boots, and a black shirt. His black hair was shoulder-length. He said a pleasant hello, then sat down in a chair and played his flute. The music was gentle, hypnotic, inviting—a meditation. It drew us in. After about ten or fifteen minutes of playing, he stopped.

"I welcome you to my home. I would like to hear from each of you a little bit about yourself and what you want from this experience."

We began one by one.

"My husband is a very sick man, and I am concerned about him," I told him when it was my turn. "I am also a healer and have done study in this area."

When we all said what we needed to say, Vernon talked to us all generally.

"There is a balance between the spiritual and corporeal worlds, and it is very important to maintain that balance," he began. "Our ancestors lived with balance between the intuitive and the intellectual—heart and mind. Our corporeal world has shifted all to the mind, and so we are like babies, learning to walk with our intuitive gifts. Before we go to the sweat lodge, my wife will explain what that will be like while I go and prepare."

Marion entered.

"The sweat lodge for us is a way to purify ourselves physically and spiritually. We believe that we sweat away illness, unhappiness, and negativity and invite in helping spirits with prayer and song," she said. "You must take off anything with metal in it before you enter. This includes rings, glasses, or any clothing that might contain metal. Women may not take part if they are having their period because, during that time, they are open to the earth, able to receive that wisdom. My older daughter will not take part today for that reason. Women must also wear long dresses or skirts."

I looked down at my jeans and back to her, questioning.

"I have some extra dresses for those who might need them," she said with a smile.

"The opening of the lodge is low, and you will have to enter on your hands and knees. Crawl around to the back as far as you can go, then sit with legs stretched out in front of you. I have towels for those who did not bring them."

When we were ready, we were shown out into the backyard, in the middle of which was a large, canvas-covered, dome-shaped structure. Next to it was an outdoor fire pit in which large round stones, about the size of a man's head, were heating in the flames. A man tended the fire, focused on his task.

I kneeled and crawled through the opening and then around to find my place. The floor was packed earth, and in the center was another fire pit. Vernon was already there, dressed only in a pair of shorts, along with his younger daughter and another Native. His wife joined when we were all inside.

Then the fire keeper lifted the flap on the doorway and passed in a pitchfork on which were placed four, glowing, red stones. Vernon helped to place these in the pit, using a strong stick. The fire keeper returned with more and more stones until the pit was filled with red-hot rocks. Then the flap over the opening was closed, leaving us in darkness except for the red glow from the rocks.

"There are four rounds," Vernon explained. "The first is an invocation where we call in the presence of sacred powers. In the second round, we all talk and pray out loud at the same time, telling the spirits what we are grateful for and what we are asking of them. In the third round, there may be messages for people, and in the fourth, we say prayers of thanks for all we have received."

Then Vernon, his daughter, wife, and the other Native man began to sing and chant as they played drums. Vernon sprinkled water on the rocks. Steam rose. He periodically dropped in small quantities of herbs, which lit and then rose in sparks within the smoke. The chanting drew me into its rhythm. We were all sweating.

It was time for round two, and everyone called out their gratitude and prayers. Vernon encouraged us all to speak loudly, so the spirits and powers would hear. The space felt holy to me. The only light was from the glow of the rocks, and the air was filled with the smoke and scent of the herbs and special plants mixed with steam. The sound of our voices raised together unified us.

During round three, there was more singing and chanting,

and then Vernon began to speak. He had general messages for the whole group that echoed his earlier message of connecting with our intuitive selves within the larger world we live in. He then had specific messages for two people only. I was one.

"You must live with integrity as a healer," he said directly to me. "You must also know that many of your peers will not understand and will stand in opposition to you—even family. You must have faith in your path and must protect yourself as a healer."

Then he added, "You must always keep one stone for yourself. That is your medicine. Medicine can be in many forms, birdsong, a smile, a quiet place, a hawk that you see in the sky. But you must always keep one stone for yourself. As for your husband, it is not your role to determine his path in this life."

His voice was strong and his words were arrows into my heart. They mingled with the sweat, the red glow, and the scent of sage.

"We are like leaves floating down a stream, sometimes sailing smooth, sometimes getting caught," he said. "Each leaf makes its own journey. You must have faith that your husband will be healed as he is meant to be healed. You must turn away from him and walk away, praying the prayer of faith for him, and in doing that—in that act—you will let him go and help him heal."

I was stunned.

This is what I came to Sedona for.

The fourth round came. Again, there was singing and chanting with the drums as the rocks continued to steam. We were directed to give thanks to spirit for all that we received. All voices responded, each in our own language. It felt like completion, closure.

The flap was raised, and cool air rushed in. Slowly, we moved and one by one crawled out into the cool night air. A man gave me his hand to steady me as I stood up. I moved toward the house, feeling that I had in some way been fundamentally changed.

Inside we found that his wife had prepared tacos—enough for an army. When I asked, the night before, what the charge would be for the sweat lodge, I was told there was no charge.

"Just bring some food to share with everyone."

I had brought a watermelon, and it complemented the meal. I also found a way to leave some money even though the ceremony was clearly an offering to us.

When I returned to the timeshare, I was still feeling the spell of the evening, I finally lay down, and when I closed my eyes, I saw plants, rocks, and flowers as I had seen them on my walk that morning. But the colors were intensified and almost liquid as though there was a layer of pure clear water over them.

The next morning, I told Earle about the sweat lodge experience and told him what Vernon had said.

"Earle, that is what I am going to do. I am going to turn my back and walk away, praying in faith that you will be healed as you are meant to be healed."

He looked startled but said nothing.

"You will be healed as you are meant to be healed," I repeated.

"That's interesting," he said quietly, almost tentatively.

We sat comfortably for the rest of the morning and into the early afternoon, talking when we wanted to, being quiet when we needed to. It felt very peaceful. The doors and windows were closed, but suddenly, I felt a wind rush through the room even though nothing moved, and I knew he was well.

Vernon's message proved to be profound. It became a guidepost for me as my husband and I moved through the two years that we had left together.

After Earle's death, I continued visiting Sedona once a year, still drawn to the big skies, the quality of air, the space, the connection with Native American culture. I began painting the amazing skyscapes as well as plant life. I hiked.

"You always look so peaceful, rested, and happy when you get back from Sedona," a friend remarked on my return from one visit. I was aware of the inner change.

Again, I was led. In 2015, retired and widowed, I decided to sell my house in York, Pennsylvania, where I had moved after my husband died, and move to Sedona. By then I had lived in York for about six or seven years, where I had busied myself with a variety of activities, including being president of the York Art Association. I woke up one morning and thought, *There's something wrong with this picture. I feel like I am at work.* I had found busyness, joined a church, dated a few men who seemed like they might be compatible, but who were not, and lost sight of myself. All I knew was that I had to leave a place in which I found things to do but no nourishment for my soul. I remembered how I felt in Sedona. There I was fed by the space, light, energy of the red rocks, and always a sense of peace. I had never been afraid to venture into new places, beginning with my trip to Europe when I was nineteen, and Sedona was not really a new place. I had been there with my husband and later with friends. And so, when I felt it was time to make a change in my life, I just did it. I was unfettered, my children were married, self-supporting, and had children of their own. I was free to take care of my own needs.

I downsized my belongings, donating all my work-related books to the university where I had worked, selling pieces of furniture that I no longer needed or used, and took boxes of other belongings to thrift shops. I talked my sister into making the cross-country trip to share driving with the promise of paying for her flight back to her home in Pennsylvania. It was a long drive, taking almost a week, but we survived each other and mostly enjoyed the adventure.

I rented a three-bedroom house on the edge of a national

forest and knew I had found my special place. A sliding-glass door off the bedroom, the large picture window in the dining room, and the back porch all looked out over pine, juniper, red rock, prickly pear cactus, and ocotillo. I love ocotillo. They have long, wavy stems and in the spring grow red, tubular flowers on the ends. I could walk off my porch and travel about forty feet across wide slabs of red rock and be on the forest trail on my way up an easy slope to the top of a hill from which I could see the Mingus Mountains. I wanted animals nearby. They seemed shy. I put out some shallow trays of seed for the ground-feeding birds and soon more and more came. It became my belief, my knowing, that they knew my house and yard were a safe place. As time went on, I became surrounded by wildlife. Coyotes crossed my yard and peed on my bushes, and I sometimes saw javelinas over on the forest trail. One morning, I felt something watching me through the curtains on the bedroom doors and found a curious mule deer, just standing there, gazing at me.

I grew to love Gambel's quail. I don't think they are at the high end of the intelligence scale, but they always made me laugh. They are ground feeders and travel in groups, clucking at each other constantly. They also have a top knot that stands straight up. Their chicks look like tiny, brown puffballs scurrying after the adults. Desert cottontails romp through the yard. I saw two behaviors that puzzled me. One was a pair of cottontails just jumping straight up and down, facing each other. Wikipedia told me they were jumping for joy. That is how it looked to me. I could almost see smiles on their faces. On another day, a single cottontail dug a very deep hole just outside of my dining room window. It got deep enough for him to sit with his entire body in the hole. I thought perhaps he was hot and needed a cooling-off place, but the next morning the hole was filled, and it looked as though it had never been dug. There was absolutely no trace of displaced earth or grasses. I was very puzzled by that and still am. Chipmunks, ground squirrels, and rock squirrels shared seed with a wide variety of birds including scrub jays, mourning doves, cardinals, finches, sparrows, and others. Hummingbirds enjoyed the feeder I hung from a porch beam. In the quietness of this country, I am enfolded by the natural world. I can see and hear the rhythm of nature, unspoiled.

What I find in this amazingly beautiful red-rock country is perspective. One can see the progression of geological change in the layers of the rock formations. It took sixty million years for this beauty to be created as winds, water, and volcanic activity sculpted the land. Human and nonhuman alike are shaped by interacting with unpredictable forces. I have come to understand that permanence and equilibrium are not absolutes and that, like the rock, I am continually being shaped.

My home in Sedona was isolated and although I loved it and was making friends in the community, I found the evenings long. When I had a need to call family back East, they were already in bed. I began to feel the loneliness settle in as the long days of winter approached. I needed company.

And so, I rescued a newly retired racing greyhound named Maggie. Or she rescued me. I went to a foster home filled with eight greyhounds. They are big animals. Maggie came to me, put her head on my knee, looked up, and the deal was made. She was part of my life for six years and was my spirit animal. We bonded. I felt eventually that we could read each other's minds. The attachment was stronger than I had felt with any of the many other dogs I had loved. She gave her heart to everyone she met just as she did to me.

I joined groups involved in conservation of the area. I became a side walker in a program for riding for the handicapped. I volunteered to train as a ranger for the Forest Service Ranger Station in Oak Creek just outside of Sedona. My training included the V Bar V Heritage Site, known to archaeologists since the mid-1940s and becoming part of the US Forest Service heritage sites in 1994. I was drawn to the mystery of the place and visited whenever I could. The distance from the small V Bar V visitor center to the actual site is an easy half-mile walk. The flat, graded path leads past areas of open meadow on the left. On the right is Wet Beaver Creek along which groves of sycamore, cottonwood, and willow grow. This lush riparian transition zone is also home to desert shrubs as well as piñon and juniper. It is thought that the rich, well-watered area attracted the Southern Sinagua community who lived and farmed here from AD 1150 to 1400, predating the rise of the Pueblo people.

The walk is peaceful, with the sound of trickling water from the creek, the hum of insects, and occasional calls from a variety of bird life. No matter how often I visit, I always feel transported into sacred space. Four huge sandstone panels stand upright, part of the cliff that reaches higher than I can see. One thousand and thirty-two individual petroglyphs have been identified here. One panel has been extensively studied. It is nearly vertical and closely aligned to true north. A full-year cycle of light and shadow was carefully tracked and documented by archaeologists, and it was discovered that sun daggers fell on specific images as the days and seasons passed, appearing to signal times for planting of certain crops. It is thought that these panels are a solar calendar and were probably attended by shamans as there are no dwelling sites close to this formation.

One morning, I arrive early. Visitors have not yet appeared. It is very quiet with sun and shadows just beginning to play across the figures on the cliffs. They seem to dance and move. As always, I marvel at the images so carefully defined in the rock, telling a story that was understood by the makers but only guessed at now. Suddenly, I feel the presence of holy people. They are standing at the foot of the cliffs. There are six. They are dressed in animal skins and are moving, celebrating, reverent, fully absorbed. I think I hear chanting. They don't notice me. It is as though the places in the rock that guide the sun allow me into a place that I know. These people were visible to me for perhaps four or five minutes. The awareness of the sacred, the moment in time that was not my time, the stillness, and the singing voices are with me still.

The magic that wove around and through me in the years I lived in Sedona touched many parts of me. In my time as a side walker for the handicapped riding program, I always worked with one horse, a mare. I came into the paddock one morning to collect her and bring her to the barn to brush and saddle her for the day. As I stepped into the paddock, she picked up her head and walked perhaps thirty feet straight to me, stopping with her face close to mine, quiet, attentive, waiting. I felt totally connected to this animal. We "knew" each other. A woman who was one of the owners was with me and she looked on in amazement. "I never saw her do that with anyone," she said.

I was working on a painting of a morning sky that had amazed me on an early walk with Maggie. Whenever she heard me say, "I need to take a picture," she stopped still. The painting turned out to be rather large, 36 inches by 48 inches, and took a long time to finish. There were times when I was painting when it felt like it was not my hand holding the brush. I was within the painting, allowing.

On a summer evening just after sunset, I saw storm clouds collecting over the mountains. It was monsoon season, and I knew there would be an electrical show. I turned off all the lights in the house and pulled a chair up in front of the large dining room window to watch the storm unfold. Maggie lay quietly on the floor next to me. The storm built and built, and the lightning lit up the sky as thunder rolled in behind. It seemed to go on for a long while, and suddenly I was "out there" in the clouds and thunder and wind and lightning, way beyond houses or people or any human habitation. I can feel it still. It was an amazing feeling to be held within nature as it happened naturally, within its own world. I felt as though I was traveling far distances. I was there for a long time, being filled, safe.

Laura Hope-Gill has written a poem, in a book called *The Soul Tree* which seemed to fit my time here. It is called "The Rock and the Rainbow."

The Bible
Is best read
In nature where

Covenants bind
Eye to land
And land to what's unseen

In all things
Heavy and weightless.
Hymns are unbroken here

And vary from tree to
Cliff composing color.
The soul shines, rains and rises

To its own many
Musics here and like a rock
Face darkened by time

Lifts itself to light.

Once more I was led. A time came when I knew I would leave the magic of Sedona and its thin places. My children, grandchildren, and sister and her family were all on the East Coast. Traveling to visit once or twice a year, adding in the logistics of work, expense, and childcare were real. I carry the friends and memories of my time there in my heart.

I moved back to Pennsylvania to an area where my sister lived. A friend that I met after the move told me about a man-made lake nearby that was surrounded by hills and hiking trails. She said that eagles, attracted by the abundance of fish in the lake, had been making a nest high in the trees halfway up such a hill. We began visiting the nest weekly to watch the development of the newly hatched eaglets which could be seen at first by binoculars, then with the bare eye as they grew big enough to peek over the edge of the nest. It was a lovely spring, and I grew to love that lake, hiking over most of the trails and admiring the waterfowl attracted to the smooth waters. My time there predated the publication of the book, *The Hidden Life of Trees* by Peter Wohlleben, and I sometimes wonder if his carefully researched book would have in any way altered or enhanced an experience that happened there.

It was a warm summer morning, and I decided to go to the lake and do some hiking on my own. My intention was to see if I could find the eagle nest although the young ones had already grown and gone. The wind was still as I walked the mile or so of worn path around the lake. It was a peaceful morning during the week with very few people on the trail. I came to the right, uphill turn toward the nest. I was used to the climb and moved easily upward. The sun was filtering in through the thick canopy of trees, leaving trails of lovely light. I had my camera with me as always and thought the opportunity to capture the path behind me as I was climbing would probably be special with the light streaming through the leaves and branches of tall trees and the lake sparkling at the bottom of the hill.

I stopped and turned around and was taken in by an experience that lasted minutes, perhaps three to five. What I saw when I looked down the hill were all the trees, moving. They were moving in place, almost dancing. I was transfixed, unafraid. I just stood still and waited and watched. Then I "heard" a message. There were no words or sounds, but I felt the trees were wanting to tell me something. It felt as though they were saying, "We are equal. We are all the same in this world." I felt their strength and authenticity. They were live beings, and I felt greeted and included and accepted. I just stood quietly. It felt as though they were reaching out to me physically. It was an utterly sacred experience. I was fully present in the moment, fully aware. I felt that I was receiving a gift. And then all was suddenly back to me, standing on the hillside looking at a lovely scene.

In Native American cultures many elders believe that all animals are relatives. I have been part of ceremonies at a time when I lived in Arizona, where the morning prayers are said to the four directions, sprinkling sacred tobacco on the earth and at each corner blessing all that lives and all that grows in this world. The two-leggeds, the four-leggeds, those that fly in the air and crawl on the ground, the sky above, the earth below, and all things growing. Perhaps I was influenced by my experiences there. But Wohlleben writes, with carefully annotated research, that trees communicate with each other, take care of each other, live in community, and have ways of protecting themselves against danger.

Recently, our neighborhood ladies group met for our monthly breakfast get-together. We no longer stand as tall as saplings; some have a twisted branch or two. I was the oldest, the youngest was sixty-five, and the rest in their seventies, all of us with various aches and pains which are always thoroughly discussed. We became friends because of proximity, and I sometimes think I would not have chosen these people as friends. Then I heard the more adult part of my brain reminding me of my tendency to judge and at that moment I remembered the trees, telling me, "We are all the same." Our group mirrored Wohlleben's description of the life of trees. My neighbors and I live rooted in community. We talk with each other, often daily, we look out for each other, support each other, often share resources, and protect each other from harm. I hear the words. We are all the same. The wisdom of the trees. And then I remembered the tree in my backyard, so many years ago, in McAllen, Texas. The tree that invited me into the backyard one soft evening to feel the embrace of a living being at a time when I was alone.

I could not stay away from the Southwest for very long and in 2016 I spent a week in Taos, New Mexico, along with a dozen or so other people who were part of a workshop focusing on indigenous cultures and healing practices. One of the leaders, Pat McCabe (Woman Stands Shining), was Navajo but, as she explains it, was trained by the spiritual elders of the Lakota Sioux. As I remember, there was a grandmother that made that connection for her. Pat would be leading two sweat lodges during the week, and she announced one morning that we would be going to the banks of the Rio Grande which ran in a rift through this part of New Mexico. The site was ten miles north of Taos. We piled into cars and drove down to the bank of the river where Pat instructed us to look only for volcanic stones as they were the only kind that would withstand the heat of the fires without exploding. The stones, after being heated to red-hot temperatures, would be deposited in a pit inside the sweat lodge. We all scrambled over the hillside, picked up rocks, and then checked with Pat to make sure they were the right ones. I finally found one that was the size of a football and carried it to her. She gave a thumbs-up and suddenly the rock I was holding began to vibrate strongly. "It's vibrating," I almost shouted to her. She just smiled. *The stones*, I thought. *My stones*. The stones that I have collected all my life, connecting me, anchoring me, as they were doing now.

In my years of gaining skills and knowledge, I stumbled into harder places of understanding energy. The Gettysburg National

Military Park, part of the US Park Service, is in the lovely town of that name. It is only about forty-five miles from my home in Pennsylvania and I have been there twice, first with family and then with guests from out of town. I cannot go there again. As I toured the beautiful rolling countryside, I began to hear cries of wounded and dying soldiers. I do not remember smelling the smells of war, but I remember the sound and I cannot go there again.

During my time in Taos, at the indigenous healing workshop, I made a side trip with another participant to a bridge about ten miles north of Taos known as the Gorge Bridge or High Bridge. Pat told us it has been the site of numerous suicides, especially among young people, and attempts have been made to put in call buttons along the bridge, some netting, and in some places some higher fencing. It is a long bridge, and I walked across to get to some jewelry vendors on the other side. It was terrifying for me. I began to hear calls and cries from the water below and a strong pull to jump. It is a very deep gorge, 800 feet. I grabbed the railing, looked for the call buttons, and held on tight the whole way across. I can drive across that bridge, but I never want to walk across again.

These situations happened many years ago and probably should have just drifted away with other kinds of memories, but I've had difficulty letting go of that feeling of hearing the voices that I felt were calling to me to do something, to join them, or in some way fix the pain. I tried a variety of ways of looking at this over the years but finally, a wise, intuitive, and trusted friend of mine suggested that what might be going on is remembered sadness about issues in my own life. That resonated with me. I sat with that thought for some weeks and finally, a few mornings ago I began to feel a need to stay in my house. I needed to stay with a feeling that was bubbling up inside. I was not sure what it was about, but it felt important, and it felt like I needed to stay with it until I understood.

The feeling was dense, heavy, brown, and continued to rise in me, and then I reached a point where the word SADNESS became paramount, expelled out of that dense and swampy muck. I suddenly saw all the sadness within my life. A life that was always very busy, full, and productive. The times that were terribly sad always occurred in situations that were also busy with work, children, and other significant stresses. I gave attention to them but did not go deeper.

Now, today, I am deep in the feeling. Immersed in it. Sadness consumes me. I feel that unique pain, that deep soul ache not only in my heart but in every single cell in my body. It inhabits me. I live in that space of feeling for hours and then begin to understand. I revisit my sad times and see that I had put each one in a box and set it on a shelf in my mind to be dealt with some other time. Current terminology labels this compartmentalization. Many people find this helpful in coping with trauma or stress, allowing one to survive the most difficult times in life.

Three images surface for me as I struggle up out of the brown swamp. I remember first my mother's stories. Her oldest sister died at the age of eighteen of tuberculosis. My mom was then thirteen. Her oldest brother fell ill with polio and Mom tells of her mother, massaging his little legs every day to try and keep his muscles mobile. Her second-oldest brother developed mastoiditis and was dangerously ill with that. Then he developed rheumatic fever. Her littlest brother died at home at the age of two from unknown causes. And her younger sister died at fifty of breast cancer. She tells me that her brothers called her "fatty" (even though I have never seen a picture of her in which she looked fat), and they pointed out that they left school early to work so she could finish high school. As she told these stories, I felt sad for her. What pain and confusion she must have felt as a little girl in a home with parents, who, although loving, were locked in their own survival story. I ached for that child who became my mother. I could not change her circumstances.

The second deep sadness that bubbles up is my father's long years with Parkinson's disease. He was a tall man, a natural athlete. He loved to work with his hands. He sketched and drew pictures and designed furniture that he built with the plans in his head. As he deteriorated over the many years of this illness, I watched as he and my mother struggled with the changes in his body and in their lives. My husband and I drove from our home in Memphis, Tennessee, to Allentown, Pennsylvania, as often as we could to bring our energy to them. I remember so very clearly that it took half of our drive back home before I was able to move out of the sadness I felt for both. I wanted to be able to help, to change their circumstance, and I couldn't.

The last sadness was wrapped around my husband's long decline. I loved him. We were partners. He was in many ways my mentor as I developed the university program I was called to in Texas. He laughed and teased and helped me see what I thought were difficult situations were not as I had fabricated them, allowing me to laugh as well. He supported me in my interests, presented me with flowers on special days or when he saw that I was having a hard day at work, and was always there in hard times.

Along with this part of our journey, many rocks and stones rose in our path. Illnesses appeared. Prostate cancer and radiation treatment when he took early retirement. A year later renal cell carcinoma resulting in loss of his right kidney. Along the way, three motorcycle accidents, an unexplained mass on his lung, and deteriorating liver from his addiction to alcohol. Other addictions to spending and eating further complicated the journey. And finally, slow cognitive decline from a mild stroke followed by multi-infarct dementia. Through all of this, I was the chair of a university program, teaching a full load. I was aware that I was grieving through this long journey but was continuously distracted by multiple other needs.

However, there was a time during his last year, sitting in

church for a Christmas Eve service, I had a vision in which I saw us spiritually separating with him traveling one path and me another. It was a very clear image, and I found that I was at peace with what I saw. I had detached. I remembered Vernon Foster's guidance about simply praying a prayer for healing for my husband in the way that was best for him. It was enough to support me at the time of his death at sixty-eight to say no to every health professional who came into his hospital room suggesting ways they could keep him alive. And it was enough when I lay beside him on the bed as he left. But I see now in the pockets of brown sludge-like sadness that hid in me, I still carried remnants of that sadness.

When I emerge from this day of letting go, I feel washed clean in every part of my being.

I see that all the other responsibilities of life in this world we live in allowed me no time to find the space that allowed me to see that I could not change one bit of anyone's life.

I went to a celebration-of-life service held recently for the life of the ninety-eight-year-old father of a friend of mine. The pastor in his comments remembered how this person was held and remembered by the thousands of people he had touched in his life. I needed to hear that to remember that every person who died at Gettysburg or Taos or in any other war or catastrophe of life is held in the hearts of those who loved them. They are loved and held in spirit. It is not my responsibility.

Three Easters. Three experiences. All different. All profound.

1956. Fifteen years old. First experience with Christ in a Lutheran church in Allentown, Pennsylvania. Wrapped in a shimmering space beyond space, together with Him, present with Him. The shimmering light filling me, all my cells. For some time after, I consider a contemplative life.

2007. Sixty-six years old. Easter in an Episcopal church in

south-central Pennsylvania. Anger mixes with tears. I am singing in the choir on Easter Sunday, not long after my husband's death. It is painful for me to sing songs of jubilation and joy at Christ's rising from the dead when all I feel is my loss. It is a dark day, a dark place. I am present only with my pain.

2022. Eighty years old. Easter in the same Episcopal church. I have just resigned from two church committees, understanding at last that I am not a fit for the requirements of those efforts. I am not a linear thinker. This Easter day I choose to sit in a back pew, not in my usual midway forward on the right. It is a different feeling sitting in the back, somewhat removed from the drama of the service. The public is invited this day for a luncheon that will follow. I am alone on one side of the pew. An elderly man in a red shirt and snowy-white hair makes his way into the other half. *He must be an unhoused person, I think. I have never seen him before. He looks pleasant.* I return to the service but then consciously allow myself to be open, to allow whatever might happen on this festival day. I am relaxed, at peace. I glance to the left at some point to look at the man in the red shirt and find a person sitting between us. I recognize the robe, now a bit dirty. I recognize the bearded face and the Presence He brings to both the man in the red shirt and myself. I sit in wonder, knowing that Christ is present for both of us, the person on the street and myself, the eighty-year-old woman. Then I know that He is present for everyone. We sit together, the three of us in that pew, in peace.

My curious mind looks for connection, relationship between these three events. I find only one. The times I have experienced not only Christ, but trees moving, shamans celebrating in AD 1100, melting into a field, finding myself gloriously part of a storm cloud, or holding a vibrating rock or practicing Healing Touch in a way that connects me with my clients have been times when I was not anticipating nor expecting any kind of event. But I was always in a personal place that I can only call OPEN. I was always in a state of calm peacefulness, perhaps some would say centered. The other side of this way of being was when I was in deep pain, whether the death of my husband or the abortion in my early life. In those times my pain closed me.

Other thoughts wander through my mind. Hildegard von Bingen, especially her music, lingers in me through these many years. I remember the first time I heard her music, how it soared and flowed through my body in silver-and-gold streams. The feeling was very close to the shimmering light and flow of energy that I felt when I was fifteen. Devi Mathieu, as quoted in *Devotions, Prayers & Living Wisdom: Hildegard von Bingen*, edited by Mirabai Starr said, "The rise and fall of the melody created a sense of cradling, of embracing, a palpable feeling of acceptance for ourselves and tolerance for each other and the world outside our doors. For a few moments we became 'Karitas,' We experienced ourselves as the love that kindles life, a constant flow in and out and through all the pieces of creation." Mathieu's words absolutely capture what I feel when I listen to that music. Another writing of Hildegard, from Starr's book:

All that the earth issues forth ... is connected
and bound to God ...
The earth is at the same time mother.
She is the mother of all, for contained in her
are the seeds of all.
The earth of humankind contains all
moistness, all verdancy, all germinating
power. It is in so many ways fruitful. All
the other parts of creation come from it.
Yet it forms not only the basic raw material for humankind,
but also the
substance of the incarnation of the Word of God.

This writing could have been written, with just minor adjustments, by a member of the Native American community or could have come from the roots of Celtic spirituality or perhaps indigenous tribes in the Amazon. Respect and reverence for nature can be found in many cultures.

In all the years of my life, I have been cradled by nature. I love that word, borrowed from the singer just quoted. I have been cradled. In my walks by the creek as a child, in walks with my children, my husband, my dogs, and just by myself. Cradled by the quiet majesty of all that surrounds me, speaks to me. I have often tried to paint what I experience. Sometimes I do it well, sometimes not, but I am drawn to paint what I see. Fields, pastures, mountains, plains, the ocean. Sometimes I feel as though I become part of my painting, not knowing who is holding the brush. When I paint or write, I feel only joy. Sometimes, when I paint, I feel that my brain lights up and think that feeling must be akin to those who both sing and listen to Hildegard's music. The world I live in nourishes me. The planet nourishes me.

I think there must be some link to creativity in all that I have experienced. Openness, wonder, connections with nature, music, and the ability to ALLOW.

And then there are stranger things. In 2010, after my husband died and I moved back to Pennsylvania, I was looking for a creative anchor and went to the web. There was an online listing of groups for those looking for a place to connect. I found a writing group and asked if I could join. I was told to submit a piece of work, and they would let me know. I was a bit put off as I had sent them information about my previous work but agreed to do so. I was a bit anxious about this. What would I write? What could I write that would be a quality bit of work? I tossed that about for several days, not being able to find a starting place. Then, one night, I was wakened, it seemed, from a dream. A story began to write itself. It felt as though someone was writing this piece of work right on my brain. I heard/read it clear as a bell. In the morning I went right to my laptop, and the whole small story appeared under my fingertips exactly as I heard it. It is here:

DARK WOMAN

She is as dark as the cave that cradles her, face angled and sharp in the dim light that filters in through the small opening. The walls and ceiling are glistening, black as obsidian and moist with sea breath. She crouches in a small space made smooth by some ancient shifting of primordial rock.

Rocking slowly, arms wrapped around herself she looks down. It was a girl child. Perfect. Exquisite. Bright red membrane against the black floor the faint light just enough to see the transparent shroud. It was what she wanted. It was what she did not want. The secret held inside now lay there, quiet, unmoving.

The woman takes some scraps of cloth which she had brought with her to this place and begins to tenderly gather up that which was part of her. Her face is without expression, her movements unconsciously following the distant rhythm of the waves slapping against the rocks below. She wraps carefully, bringing a piece of cloth from bottom to top, then in from one side, then the other, finally covering the tiny face, which appears to be in peaceful sleep. As she works, a sound escapes her throat and becomes a low and ancient hymn coming from someplace inside, timeless.

Here, with sounds of breaking waves, the motion of slender arms and a sacred song, that which had been inside and part of her becomes outside and apart from her. The place in her soul where the child had begun, closes and becomes again an empty place. The woman, dark body shining with sea breath and sweat, slowly unfolds herself, picks up her bundle, and makes her way with feline grace over the rocky floor to the entrance. She bends to move through the small opening and emerges into the glittering morning sea light and chill breeze. Standing for a moment, majestic in her sharp beauty, she throws back her head and calls out her anguish to all that live, before beginning her descent to the shore below.

This writing was given to me. I made no edits. I just transcribed.

I was accepted into the group. I have no idea where the writing came from. I could guess that perhaps it was a link to my abortion decades before or from another time in which I lived. I will never know. Dreams are experienced by everyone, and most people hold them as special. They link internal with external. They are like fluid clouds, images of thoughts to be, thoughts that might be, unborn but with shape, movement, texture, waiting to be birthed in forms that we suddenly recognize as long-ago wishes.

They are expressions of us that we skirt, flirt at not knowing. Dreams tug at our sleep, at our mind's eye, at our heart's desires, waiting patiently for the opening that allows a slip through our reality, our understanding, our instant recognition.

HERE NOW

It was a humid August morning, Sunday. I woke up feeling sort of bleary, as though behind a screen. I debated on going to church and finally decided I would. Still feeling bleary. I settled into a pew, not focused on much, waiting for opening music. Suddenly I felt lifted out of my seat, almost literally, by the sound of a trumpet. A man stood in the choir stall and played a most beautiful piece of sacred music. I had not even noticed him there. Still behind my blurry screen, I suddenly felt and almost saw the vibration of the music rise from the floor, up along the walls, playing with the light coming through the stained-glass windows, then up across the high vaulted beige ceiling, meeting at the very top. It felt as though the music became a warm gentle blanket cradling everyone who sat in the nave of the church in a vibrating embrace. The music bound us together.

It is music that now carries me swiftly through the eighty years of my space in this time. I hear the church music of the Lutheran tradition in which I grew up. Even as a child, I could feel its sacred presence, although I did not have the words or concept for it then. Before I knew words, I knew the composer was expressing something very deep in his soul. I could feel it. Much later, I learned that Bach, Handel, and Graupner often wrote *Soli Deo Gloria* on their compositions. In Latin, this means Glory to God Alone. I have seen it noted that Bach said, "I play the notes as they are written, but it is God who plays the music." I suddenly find myself whisked into my painting studio as I painted an incredible morning sky that I saw in Sedona. As I painted, I remember the feeling that I did not know who was holding the brush. I have had that feeling with other paintings I have done as well. I sometimes feel that as I write. My fingers are moving on the keyboard or with pen across the page, but another voice sometimes appears as in the sudden emergence of ALLOW. Is this creative person to Creator or Creator to creative person, I wonder? Is there a connection with the word ALLOW? Do we all have this creative capacity, and in what form does it emerge? Scientific inquiry, music, art, architecture, teaching, healing? The laughter of a child's discovery, the soft singing of a mother comforting a frightened baby a creative response?

The forms of sacred and creative response that I know swirl about me like bits of white paper gliding on the wind. Mariachi music full of joy, inviting movement, my father listening to Bing Crosby crooning Christmas melodies. The blues carrying the soul of a culture, country-western wailing themes of big trucks and lost women. I remember the chants of the medicine men at the V Bar V in Arizona, church music played in denominations that were new to me, the music of a stream tumbling over and through rocks, the sound of wind in palm trees, the sound of wind in pines. It is in the music of Hildegard von Bingen that flows through my veins bringing me in touch with the Divine. We live in creation. It is ours to touch.

I see that all cultures are wrapped, bound in music, whether the forms are song, chant, rhythm, or voice. I am suddenly shifted back into church by another sound.

Brian, the trumpet player, is now chanting the psalm. It

is beautiful, his voice a clear trained tenor. Now fully back in this space, I enjoy two more musical offerings of his before the service ends with another lovely trumpet solo.

When my voice was younger and my vision clearer, I sang in the choir of this Episcopal church and grew to love the Anglican way, not so terribly different from the Lutheran forms of my first fifty years. I walk up to the front of the church after the service.

"Brian, I so much enjoyed your music, it meant a great deal to me," I said.

"Yes, with the choir not singing in the summer there is a little more freedom in how to use music in the service," he said, face relaxed, almost glowing.

"I could feel the vibration of the music," I said. It filled the church. "I believe music is healing."

"Oh yes," Brian said. "I do too. I feel it. I didn't want to stop singing. And I feel the response to the music from the people in the congregation. It becomes shared."

I was reluctant to leave this conversation, but he began to put his trumpet away and pick up his music, clearly needing to leave. We said good-bye to each other, and I said a final thank-you.

I walked out into the August sunshine, no longer bleary and no longer feeling as though I was behind a screen. A bit of my conversation with Brian played in my mind as I drove home. It was his comment about feeling a sharing, a communication with the congregation as he played and sang. A feeling of response from those hearing the music, his music.

As the days moved on, I kept finding myself pulled back to Brian's comment about feeling response from those hearing his music. When I was practicing Healing Touch, there was truly a connection between myself and the client. It was always a shared experience, a communication as was the connection with the clients I treated as an occupational therapist.

I began to think about the call-and-response form in music, wondering if there was such a connection with what I already knew, not just from forms defined by man's thought, but by nature.

I am told by others who know much more about music than I do that the call-and-response musical story began in sub-Saharan Africa as songs of connection, of rhythm, songs of community, like a conversation. They told me the call-and-response forms became part of gospel music, the blues, jazz, and hip-hop. And we hear these patterns in popular music as well. Such music invites and allows people to sing along, to be part of the conversation.

I talked to Rodney, our church organist who is also a gifted singer and teacher, about call and response and he simply said, "With call and response, only one person needs to know the melody." I laughed at that at first, taking his comment lightly, but then thought, what a profound statement. Perhaps in the world in which we live and work and play, every living creature responds in chorus to the call of our Creator, each in its own way.

I drift back to my ten years of living in Memphis, Tennessee. One of the most enjoyable things my husband and I did was walk in the evenings along Beale Street in the spring and summer. It was a place where people came to listen and sometimes sing along to the sounds of a culture pouring out of the open doors of one club after another. There was one special place, a cellar of sorts. Steps led down from street level into a dim, smoky, long room with round tables arranged at the foot of a low, wooden stage where the musicians came together to play. People sat, had drinks, leaned back in their chairs eager for the evening, their forms dimmed and blurred in the smoky blue haze. It was a place where we were held by the music long into the evening. Voice and guitar talked to each other in a relentless rhythm and then spoke to other instruments as well. Back and forth, call and response, a conversation.

Although it is now a long time ago, I still remember some tunes from my childhood that stay with me still in bits and pieces. "If you're happy and you know it, clap your hands," a repeated song with hand claps. And I loved "Alouette, gentille Alouette" as a child. I did not speak French, but the words found their way into my memory because of the lilting call-and-response tune and later "The Banana Boat Song" by Harry Belafonte. Who didn't soar along with his "Day-O, Day-O," and the answer of the chorus? I hear the patterns in contemporary music as well, such as in Bruno Mars, "Locked Out of Heaven," and Ray Charles, "Lonely Avenue."

The art form of opera brings yet another face to the power of music. In a recent discussion featuring the new opera, *The Hours* (2022), Kevin Puts, the Pulitzer Prize-winning composer and Renee Fleming, one of the three performers, spoke of opera as a living art form that relays feelings that give us hope. Fleming went on to say, "It's the music that connects everything."

I remember now, sixty-seven years ago, when my mother took me along on the church music club trip to my first opera at the New York Metropolitan Opera House. It was Mozart's *The Marriage of Figaro.* I do not remember who the singers were, but I remember the soaring soprano who sang what my mother later told me was an aria. The music, which sounded to me like a magical bird, filled me, the theater, and my imagination. I had never heard anything like that sound. The call was the music, the response was that a whole new world was opened to me.

No matter what the denomination of our myriad of places of worship, we find an order of service that is defined by the concept of call and response. However, in my experience, these are sentences that become forms of rote response as prayer or confessions of faith as they are read in every service, almost as a chanted ritual reading.

Martin Buber, the Austrian Jewish philosopher, wrote about two attitudes in human existence. The attitude of *I-It* and the attitude of *I-Thou*. This book has had a home with me on my bookshelf for decades. I-It is an attitude toward an object we use or experience. But an I-Thou attitude is one of relationship. It's one thing to respond to a beautiful sunset as an object to admire and a totally different thing to respond to a person calling you to tell you they love you. Something about the response is different because a personal relationship is involved.

Much of wildlife follows patterns of call and response. Members of bird families call each other as do dolphins and whales. Those songs have long been recorded. Bees dance directions leading hive mates to flowers, water, or new nesting sites. Insects have patterns of calling, some loud, some soft. Elephants rumble and trumpet conversations.

All life responds to changes in wind, amount of sunshine, and water. Plants respond to long, soaking rain with vibrant growth of green. Flower faces follow the sun across the sky. My mother's African violets responded to her daily soft conversations with health and continual flowering.

We live in relationship. The muscles, nerves, and blood vessels in our bodies function always in relationship to each other. People function in relationship to others in all our activities as well as to changes in the natural world. We live in relationship to smiles and hugs as well as to angry words or scowls. Calls and responses echo for each of us all day, every day. We only need to be present to what is.

As reported by the Smithsonian Institution's Human Origins Program, the human brain evolved most rapidly in complexity from two million to 800,000 years ago, in times when periods of major climate change challenged humankind. The beginning of writing is recorded as appearing approximately

5,000 years ago in ancient Egypt and Sumer, a very recent development in time.

David Leeming, in *Creation Myths of the World*, identifies over 200 creation stories, arising from cultures worldwide. They rose out of the environment in which they originated in both oral and written history, searching for answers about the unknown mystery of how all things came to be. Nearly all identify a supreme being as the starting point from which all things develop. It appears that the capacity for awe and wonder is perhaps part of our DNA.

The Book of Genesis creation story is one of these creation myths, common to both Judaism and Christianity.

> *In the beginning when God created the heavens and the earth, the earth was a formless void; and darkness covered the face of the deep while a wind from God swept over the face of the waters. Then God said: "Let there be light." And there was light. And God saw that the light was good; and God separated the light from the darkness.*
> *God called the light Day, and the darkness He called Night. And there was evening and there was morning, the first day. (New Revised Standard Version)*

The knowledge, beliefs, and rituals that we share are based on thousands of years of observing our world. Themes bind cultures. They grow from what was observed by each culture in the worlds in which they lived.

What if all creation, the world, and existence, are not just meaningless random chaos? What if creation is a song, a call to respond to? What would it look like to respond in relationship to the song we hear under our experiences of beauty, truth, love, goodness, and mercy?

My melody, the song in my heart and soul, is carried by a

truth I find in the personhood of the Christ I met at the age of fifteen and whom I saw again on Easter of 2021. It is the truth of being present with compassion and healing for every person I meet. My melody is carried by the small green anole who reaches out to touch my finger in deep south Texas, a sacred connection between species, a moment of grace. My melody echoes the drumbeats of the shamans, in AD 1100, immersed in prayers at the foot of pillars covered with petroglyphs. My melody is filled with songs of birds, streams, wind, leaves, storms, and soothing breezes. It is filled with the tree beings and their promise of their presence and their gift of saying we are equal. My melody sings in the joy of the gifts I have been given by grace. The gift of creation, the gift of seeing, the gift of living in celestial realms. My melody sings in the joy of my daughters, the laughter of my grandchildren, and the awareness of the unutterable closeness found in the passing of my husband. Legions of patients, clients, families, coworkers, teachers, and friends of all species gather around me in a great chorus of their wisdom.

I am a melody of creation, dancing with Creator.

How do 200 creation stories fit into the world in which I live? Do our stories connect? Are they similar in any way? Is the basic question the same? How can all the wonder we see be explained? Where do I come from? Am I cared for? What is my song?

One thing I begin to see and understand from Leeming's work is that each culture's unique story, growing from its environment, its geographical setting, its climate, becomes the Truth for that group. The beliefs held by each group, the story that is created over time, small piece by small piece, built in relationship, is the Truth for that group. My Truth, my values, my melody, were shaped by the immigrant community who found their way to a small city in southeastern Pennsylvania.

The sense of support and caring and Christian love were part of the Lutheran community in which they worshipped their image of a Creator who is supreme overall. I see mystery in all 200 creation stories. Unanswerable questions as to how, why, were we created. All groups try and answer those questions; they create answers, and that is perhaps what all creation is. Each of us creates from our own being every single day in the work that we do, the songs we sing, the paintings we create, the play we enjoy with our children. It is an ongoing melody, this creation story of ours, arising from our hearts, our minds, our environment. We live and create our story each day in trust and love as it flows from us. We create together with all living animals, plants, insects as all beings create from their own worlds.

Can we take that image of the Mayan Indian Circle of Friends pottery piece and expand that circle around this planet, clockwise, counterclockwise, spiral until all 200 groups are touching each other in some way, seeing that it is a touch, a held hand, eye contact that links us all. We become our own creation story, woven together in relationship, understanding our shared lives, needs, and joy in this symphonic mystery which we will never fully understand because we are still creating it.

Can we not wonder at the images from the James Webb Space Telescope over these past few years? The technology which created this telescope is the product of many, many creative minds worldwide, collaborating over decades. The world of quantum physics has been developed over the last century among scientists and astrophysicists through many countries over many years, enfolded and held in their government archives. We, in this world, on this planet, wish to find "habitable" environments in which we could live away from this planet. Would it be possible that there might be other alternatives?

The word "allow" now becomes a magic word, a mystery

word. We live our lives, shaped by what we hear and see from birth. We understand that world as given, inflexible, the way it is. But if we allow our minds and hearts to see in different ways, to open, we can hear notes that are different, perhaps strange sounding but notes that begin to create a song different from what we have always known. Notes that include us in the Mystery of Being and the Melody of Who We Are.

I live now in south-central Pennsylvania, an area of the world not yet in the throes of drought. My sister lives close by and is a master gardener whose yard is her anchor and her playground.

My younger daughter and her family are visiting from Maine. They have not been here for many years, and my sister has not seen them for decades. She has been telling me how much she misses her niece and my grandchildren.

We pull into my sister's driveway and the whole of our families meet in the yard. I am touched by seeing the pure joy and tearful happiness on my sister's face, and the same on my daughter's as they hug. "Shall we just stay in the yard?" I say, and everyone agrees as we start our tour.

I watch. My sister and my daughter quickly fall into a conversation that is just theirs, couched in a shared love of flowers and plants. I see that my daughter has a deep relationship with the plants as she touches them gently, rubbing her fingers over the leaves to catch the scent. Her touch is loving, purposeful, respectful. Conversation is filled with names: anise hyssop, comfrey, French sorrel, and ironweed. I learn that some of these are healing plants or can be eaten or are plants that pollinators love. My daughter and my sister are wrapped in their joy, their conversation, their sharing. They are in relationship, not only with each other but with nature. My two grandsons circle us tirelessly, in and out of the sunlight that finds its way through the trees. Wherever we walk they are there, swarming about us like wrens, highly energetic, totally happy in their play. Determined to enjoy every moment of their afternoon, they joust with two long, wooden swords painted silver, keeping us all safe from dragons. "Oma, please, please," my thirteen-year-old grandson runs up to me and says excitedly. "For my birthday or Christmas, or something, can I please, please have two swords like these?" He is breathless, his cheeks rosy with excitement and play. "I will see what I can do," I say, smiling. My nephew, the same age as my daughter, follows, not saying much with words but saying a great deal with the look of enjoyment on his face as he follows the energy. My brother-in-law appears from the house with a new creation of his own. A cigar-box guitar. We all gather to admire.

These are the bits and pieces of life that form a Creation story, a Truth. Shared experiences, murmurs of appreciation, laughter as dragons are slain, the songs of birds in my sister's pawpaw trees, and the sigh of wind through the leaves. This bit of story which unfolds on a sunny afternoon in this part of Pennsylvania is held in each person's mind and heart, a treasure to be passed on in conversation over years or shared perhaps in a poem or a song. A symphony of life, the notes being written as they are created.

We are the melody of Creation, dancing with Creator.

AUTHOR'S NOTE

This book emerged after eight decades of experiences that came to me unbidden. They were never frightening, always amazing but always hidden, first, because I had no one to talk to about them and later somehow felt that if I did, I would not be believed.

However, over the last several years I have felt a shift, perhaps in consciousness or perhaps within myself that now allows me to share what I have learned. I have had guides, mentors, and wise people who have contributed to my journey. Among them are: Dr. Christine Page, a most gifted and kind physician and intuitive, who taught me in a way that allowed me to see myself as someone who has gifts to offer and who has provided guidance as to how to do that. Mary Frost, a wise mentor from my days of involvement in the practice of Healing Touch, as well as many others I met on that journey, supported me. Nan Lu, OMD, shared his energy, wisdom, and positive guidance on the integration of cross-cultural healing within his books and the traditional Chinese medicine conferences he designed. Dr. Rachel Naomi Remen taught her wisdom through her books and presentations, providing me with everlasting awareness of the importance of awe and wonder in the practice of healing and wholeness. Robert Temple, in his *New Science of Heaven*, brought me clearly and carefully to a better understanding of the concept of quantum plasma, leading me further into the promise of what is beginning to be known to us on this planet and beyond.

Thirty years ago, Dr. Daniel Kennedy and Dr. Henry Vasconez, of the University of Kentucky Medical Center, each shared great wisdom within one simple sentence each that changed my life. I see now how many other teachers, physicians, and friends through the years have added to the depth of my understanding of spirit and compassion.

I have read widely and searched for more understanding as this book evolved. Some of the contributors are as follows:

Fr. Ronald Rohlheiser guided me to Joseph Cardinal Bernardin's beautiful book, *The Gift of Peace*, as the cardinal's words allowed us to walk with him toward his death from pancreatic cancer. Fr. Rohlheiser also led me to an awareness of Hildegard von Bingen, a mystic of the Middle Ages, who has shaped my life. Mary Sharrett's *Illuminations: A Novel of Hildegard von Bingen*, provided me with a rich and well-researched picture of her life, as did Mirabai Starr's edited collection of *Devotions, Prayers, and Living Wisdom: Hildegard von Bingen*.

I somehow was led to John Philip Newell's book *Sacred Earth, Sacred Soul, Celtic Wisdom for Awakening What Our Souls Know and Healing the Earth*. Newell is ordained in the Church of Scotland and is also a scholar of Celtic tradition. I found connection here with the reverence for the earth, which is also part of Native American teachings; Peter Wohlleben's *The Secret Life of Trees*, and Hildegard von Bingen's songs and poetry.

I feel deeply connected with the poetry of Ojibwe Richard Wagamese's meditation on his soul in *Embers* and Laura Hope-Gill's poem "The Rock and the Rainbow" in the book *The Soul Tree*.

Theological thought lent itself to my deeper understanding of spirit and healing through Henri Nouwen's classic *The*

Wounded Healer, and Martin Buber's *I and Thou.*

The amazing resources of the Smithsonian Institution's Human Origins program allowed me to identify and track the evolution of man's cognitive development as well as the history of written language, allowing a unique perspective on man's capacity to adjust to events beyond his control.

Julia Cameron's The Artist's Way provided a journaling tool that led me to find the importance of the word "allow," which became part of my life theme, and American Buddhist nun, Pema Chödrön, in *When Things Fall Apart*, gives us her truth in her singular clear voice.

Bits and pieces of wonderful broadcasts on NPR added texture and contemporary commentary on music forms that added greatly to my knowledge as I grew in my own melody of self.

Finally, David Leeming's two volumes of *Creation Myths of the World*, gave me a perspective allowing my expansion into a view of our world and its families as a world fully connected, living in relationship.

ACKNOWLEDGMENTS

This book would never have happened without the support, encouragement, and input from these very special people.

I am so grateful for continued support from Carolyn Flynn, Story Catalyst, through kn literary. Carolyn has been my developmental editor throughout all my work and has been an astute guide, teacher, and cheerleader. She has helped me uncover and discover the message and meaning of the words that appear on the page. She has also helped me understand the craft of writing through her feedback.

I met Douglas Brouwer one morning over breakfast at a writing conference. That meeting led to many online discussions about writing and religious ponderings. Doug is a retired Presbyterian pastor with keen interest and success in writing as well as theology. I knew I wanted to write again but was not finding clear direction. It was those many conversations and discussions that eventually showed me the way into this book I will forever be grateful to Doug for his willingness to engage in this discourse and for his patience and support.

I first heard Dr. Christine Page speak at a conference perhaps twenty years ago and have followed her writings and talks since. She is a physician as well as a gifted intuitive, author, teacher, and kind supporter for those who are seekers. She was very helpful to me in the writing of this book. She saw my own intuitive gifts and helped me understand what they were and how I could best develop and use them. A new world opened to me through her guidance. I am forever grateful.

Atmosphere Press has given me a publishing home that is amazingly supportive, responsive, and kind. Staff in all areas are quick to respond to my questions and needs. Tammy Letherer provided excellent editorial feedback, which I would not have caught on my own. Alex Kale, Managing Editor, the source for answers to all questions, allowed me to see the big picture, and with humor and kindness, shepherded me through many anxiety attacks. Ronaldo Alves, Art Director, guided the cover design process, and as with all Atmosphere staff managed me gently through my moments of indecision. From beginning to end, I cannot say enough for this gem of a publishing company.

Family, friends, and colleagues have cheered me on. Karen Jeffries and J. Ivan Ruiz, despite busy lives of their own, have given me solid feedback as readers. My cherished daughters, Mary and Katie, as well as my sister, Jane Musser, are always staunch supporters as are Rita, Karen G., and Tom Travin, editor and friend. A special thanks to Cheryl Kindt whose gentle voice helped guide me through ideas for how the inclusion of art might happen and to Lynn Keller, whose clear voice and vision also added to this discussion. And for the multitudes who joined in with their comments about cover design. All of those who surround me in my community dance with me in this work.

ABOUT ATMOSPHERE PRESS

Founded in 2015, Atmosphere Press was built on the principles of Honesty, Transparency, Professionalism, Kindness, and Making Your Book Awesome. As an ethical and author-friendly hybrid press, we stay true to that founding mission today.

If you're a reader, enter our giveaway for a free book here:

SCAN TO ENTER
BOOK GIVEAWAY

If you're a writer, submit your manuscript for consideration here:

SCAN TO SUBMIT
MANUSCRIPT

And always feel free to visit Atmosphere Press and our authors online at atmospherepress.com. See you there soon!

ABOUT THE AUTHOR

JUDITH ELIZABETH BOWEN's vision is supported by forty-two years as a registered occupational therapist and a period of practice as a Healing Touch practitioner. Both enrich her spiritual and analytical gifts as a healer. More than half of her professional life was spent in clinical practice in a wide variety of health-care settings. The remainder she spent teaching in undergraduate and graduate programs. She has been published in professional journals, a textbook, three anthologies, and two memoirs and has presented widely at national conferences and workshops. She has also been recognized by the American Occupational Therapy Association as a Fellow for her achievements. A native of Pennsylvania, she now devotes her time to creating. Writing, painting, and continued learning and growth fill her life as do her children, grandchildren, and friends.